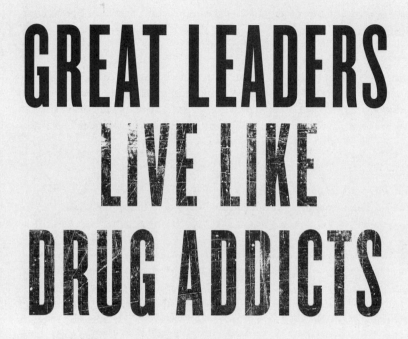

**Author Note**

First, this is not a book for addiction treatment. If you are struggling with addiction, get help immediately. If you are living in the U.S., you can visit www.samhsa.org or call 211 (www.211.org) for help.

Second, in terms of the content in this book: Over the course of my recovery—nearly two decades—I have learned so much, from recovery meetings and literature to business training and books to mentors, speeches, podcasts, and so on. My goal in this book is to integrate everything I have learned and turn it into a simple and actionable program for the reader. I have been influenced by so much wisdom from so many places that it's nearly impossible for me to track the slogans and terms I have used here and the sources from which they came. If something that is not mine appears here, I am in no way trying to pass it off as my own. I am grateful for the influence of the content I have received over my lifetime, and I see my value more in how I have systematized that wisdom and applied it in a unique way. All props and respect go to those who came before me.

Finally, my stories are to the best of my recollection. As a drug addict who ingested quite a few chemicals over my lifetime, there is a decent chance my brain has remembered some details incorrectly.

ISBN: 978-1-948677-31-8
ISBN: 978-1-948677-32-5 (eBook)
ISBN: 978-1-948677-53-0 (audio)

Published by Forefront Books.

Cover Design by Bruce Gore, Gore Studio Inc.
Interior Design by Bill Kersey, KerseyGraphics

Printed in the United States of America
20 21 22 23 24 25 5 4 3 2 1

# GREAT LEADERS LIVE LIKE DRUG ADDICTS

## HOW TO LEAD LIKE YOUR LIFE DEPENDS ON IT

## MICHAEL BRODY-WAITE

# DEDICATION

To my fellow human beings: The labels of "leader" and "addict" have historically been reserved for a certain subset of our society. I wrote this book so that you can see how both of these separate concepts intersect inside of you and, more importantly, why that gives you the power to change the world.

To my fellow addicts in any form: Those of us in recovery are the ones who give me the most strength, but it is those of us who are still out there that give me the most hope.

To my higher power whom I choose to call God: I don't know why you guided me to leave you out of this text, but I believe you are still on every page.

# CONTENTS

# INTRODUCTION

NOBODY EVER LOOKS AT A DRUG ADDICT AND SAYS, "MAN, THAT GUY really has it all together. I wish I could be more like him." You've probably never heard a high-power CEO or business-training guru hold up a drug addict as an example of quality leadership. So what gives with the title of this book? Why on earth would I title my very first book *Great Leaders Live Like Drug Addicts?*

As you'll find out, I know what I'm talking about when it comes to drug addicts. I spent years of my life pumping as much poison into my system as I could. I was an unemployable, homeless, thieving, lying drug addict. How's that for authenticity?

But you'll also learn that I know what I'm talking about when it comes to great leaders. I've been clean for seventeen years, and in that time, I've been a leader in retail, corporate America, startups, nonprofits, and as an entrepreneur. I am an award-winning, three-time CEO, and I've taken a startup from nothing to 20,000 percent growth and a subsequent eight-figure acquisition by a publicly traded company.

I've been at the very bottom, and I've spent time at the top. I've sat with drug addicts in more than two thousand twelve-step meetings, and I've sat with billionaire businesspeople around mahogany conference tables. And, in that time with both these groups—*and this is where I get controversial*—I've learned that the same things drug addicts do that makes them outcasts from society are what leaders do in their effort to become "great."

## LIVING IN ADDICTION

Growing up, I learned that being an addict was a terrible thing, that there was a deep stigma associated with addiction. So when I *became* an addict, I was ashamed. I did everything I could to hide that part of me from the world. Drug addicts who are using are in what we call *active addiction*. And, as my active addiction grew worse and I couldn't stop, I continued to lie and hide in order to get what I wanted. I developed tunnel vision; I was so focused on getting what I wanted that I often didn't see the impact I was making on the people I loved or even myself. And, sometimes when I *could* see it, I just didn't care. When my family and friends finally intervened, I yelled and screamed at them like they were crazy. I protested. I stomped my feet. I proclaimed, "I don't have a problem!" I'd been throwing up blood but I honestly believed I was doing fine. I just couldn't see it. I had spun so many lies I couldn't keep up with what was real and what was fake. Even at rock bottom, I was doing my best to show everyone around me how well-off I was. If you had told me to be *real* or to be my *true self* in my days of active addiction, I wouldn't have known what you were talking about. The lies I told myself and others had become such a big part of my identity that I couldn't see which parts of me were real and which were fake.

Over the years, I have been taught that an addict is someone who does the same thing over and over again, despite negative consequences.

So after watching endless politician and CEO scandals play out in public and after coaching thousands of leaders in dozens of fields, my observation is that most leaders learn to act a lot like addicts in active addiction. Sure, leaders may not be facing the same kind of *immediate* dangers that I did back then, but you'd be surprised how real the danger is for these overworked and overstressed professionals. Most of the leaders I talk to tell me how tired they are, how little free time they have, and how seldom they take a day off to hang out with their families and friends or pursue hobbies without thinking about work. No matter how hard they work, no matter how much success they achieve, they never truly feel successful enough and always believe they need more. They chase the results they want, whether it's a promotion, more power, a raise, a big team, or the corner office, going out of their way to bury their true selves behind a mask of what they think others expect them to be. They work long hours, forsaking their families, friends, and personal lives. They make decisions they regret because they're scared of losing out or not getting something they want. They feel pressured to project a level of calm control over their responsibilities and teams. They hide their weaknesses and cover up their mistakes—hiding their *humanity* in the process. They end up becoming so laser focused on their goals that they become blind to the problem, doing almost anything to get their fix.

One addict is hiding their true self on the journey to destitution or death; the other addict is hiding their true self on the journey to success.

## THE HOPE SHOT

As a drug addict, I didn't know there was another way. I was vaguely familiar with recovery, but I thought that was just a punishment. No one ever told me that my addiction, what I believed to be the *worst* thing about me, could somehow become the *best* thing about me. I had no idea that I would one day find myself speaking in front of thousands of people declaring that I wasn't successful in *spite of* the fact that I'm a drug addict; I was successful *because* I'm a drug addict.

Same thing for leaders. Sure, we have heard of authentic leadership, but these days that appears to be more of a fantasy than a reality. Not all leaders are able to relate to having a drug addiction, but most can relate to the belief that the worst thing about them is something they need to hide from the world, especially if they want to be a great leader. And whether you are a business leader, an individual contributor, a stay-at-home parent, or something else, *everyone* is responsible for leading *someone*. The problem is, we have become so focused on leading *others*, we have fundamentally lost the ability to lead *ourselves*.

The reason I wrote this book is twofold: As a drug addict, I learned that there was another way to be an addict that no one had ever showed me, a way not just to *survive* being an addict but to *thrive* as an addict. As a leader, I'm here to tell you that there is also another way to lead. Another way to be great that goes against everything we have ever learned. A way to lead that revolutionizes the rules of leadership.

## LIVING IN RECOVERY

Addicts *use* all the time or we don't use at all; it's all or nothing. That's the same attitude we have to have in recovery. We either keep a recovery mindset and do recovery diligently, or we fall right back into our addiction. Our life literally depends on our ability to do the work every day. I will be a drug addict the rest of my life. That's who I am. But every day I have a choice: I can choose active addiction or I can choose recovery. I got clean on September 1, 2002, and I have chosen recovery every day since. But if I stop doing what drug addicts do to recover, I'll end up doing what drug addicts do to die. It's that simple.

What I'm going to share with you in this book is how I learned true, authentic leadership. I didn't get it from an MBA, college, or leadership seminar. Instead, I got it by fighting for my life in my battle against addiction. When I learned how to become a *recovering* addict, I didn't just learn how to live; I learned how to do the most important thing any leader can do: lead myself. And when you start truly leading yourself with no lies, no deception, no excuses—*no masks*—then you'll start leading the people around you differently. You won't just be the kind of leader people want to *have*; you'll be the kind of leader people want to *be*.

This isn't your ordinary leadership book. You won't find ten steps to improve efficiency or five secrets for boosting your bottom line. And yes, there are books that talk about *what* authenticity is and *what* the benefits are. However, those books aren't showing people *how* to actually achieve this goal, *how* to implement systematic changes in their lives and leadership. When I walked into rehab, my counselors and therapists didn't just talk about *what* I needed to do; they showed me *how* to do it. That's what I want to do for you now.

> If I stop doing what drug addicts do to recover, I'll end up doing what drug addicts do to die.

I have taken everything I learned in recovery and everything I learned as a successful leader and CEO over nearly two decades and developed a program that teaches any leader a new way to live and a new way to lead. In this book, I will unpack the process that helps millions of addicts around the world stop hiding what they think is the worst thing about themselves and turn it into the best thing about themselves. Then I will show you something we haven't seen before: a program that creates great leaders by allowing them to stop hiding who they are, teaches them how to remove the masks they are wearing, and unlocks their secret weapon—their true selves. It's called the

Mask-Free Program, and it's not only going to change the way you lead, it's going to change the way you live.

**My goal with this book is to screw up your leadership.**

As we say in recovery, "A head full of recovery will screw up your using." Well, my goal with this book is to screw up your leadership. In a world where so many of our leaders are doing the same thing that active drug addicts do, I want to show you that, if you follow a similar process to the one that helps addicts recover, you can stop hiding who you are behind a mask and lead in a fundamentally different way that makes you *truly great*.

You get to choose: you can be a leader who hides who they are just like an active drug addict, or you can be a leader who shows their true self just like a recovering drug addict. Either way, you'll find out why great leaders really do live like drug addicts.

# CHAPTER 1

# I'M MIKE. I'M A DRUG ADDICT.

I'M SURE YOU REMEMBER YOUR FIRST "REAL" JOB. THE NERVOUSNESS. The commitment. The determination to do everything just right to make the most of the opportunity you'd been given. I started that first job back in college. I spent so much time perfecting my role that my grades suffered, and I was eventually kicked out of school for it. I bet all the money I had on this job, which led to me going broke and getting kicked out of my apartment. I poured everything I had into this job with laser focus twenty-four hours a day, seven days a week with no breaks. Despite all the success I've had in the years since then, I still identify myself by the first real job I ever had. To this day, whenever I'm around a new group of people, I still introduce myself by that very first job title:

Hi. I'm Mike. I'm a drug addict.

Let me give you a picture of my normal "day at the office" back then. I was at Venice Beach at 2:00 in the morning sitting with a homeless guy on one side and a prostitute on the other. It was a weird triangle of lies and manipulation. I wanted the homeless man's *blunt* (a hollowed-out cigar filled with weed). He wanted the prostitute. The prostitute wanted me to be her last customer of the night. But none of us was honest about what we wanted or what we had to offer. I pretended I had money. I didn't. He pretended he had more weed. He didn't. And she pretended her flirting wasn't an attempted business transaction. It was. All three of us were working overtime pretending to be someone else. That was probably the biggest lesson I learned as an addict: how to be whoever I needed to be in order to get what I wanted.

This is a behavior I lived and breathed during my years as an active drug addict. It's also a behavior I've seen nearly every day since—but I'm not talking about something that's only hiding in back-alley drug deals or condemned crack houses. No, this is something I've seen most often out in the "civilized" world of business. We live in a world where most leaders hide behind masks to get what they want. As a result, the rest of us learn to do the same. Then, before we know it, nearly everyone is a "mask addict," hiding who we truly are time and time again.

> **That was probably the biggest lesson I learned as an addict: how to be whoever I needed to be in order to get what I wanted.**

I realize it may feel like a stretch to compare drug addiction to mask addiction, to make the claim that practically everyone is addicted to some sort of mask. Well, we know that most addicts remain addicts when they live in denial and refuse to see their problem. So in order to determine if you are a mask addict, I am going to start by showing you what addiction looks like through my own story. Then I will show you what it looks like to be a mask addict and why knowing that can give you a significant advantage. Ultimately, you will see how the world of drug addiction and the world of leadership have some stark similarities that most of us would rather ignore. I can't ignore them anymore and by the time you finish reading this book, neither will you.

We're off to a great start, huh? You've probably never picked up a leadership book that used the terms *drug addict, prostitute, blunt,* and *crack house* and then had the gall to suggest you are an addict too—all in the first few pages. If that didn't tip you off, let me clear it up for you right off the bat: this is not your standard, boring, vanilla, paint-by-numbers leadership book. We're going to deal with some real-life stuff, some things that will probably make you uncomfortable. You're going to read about some really stupid things I've done, but you'll also hear about the process I used to turn things around. Throughout this book, I'm going to walk you through the program I've developed over the years that turned a broke, homeless drug addict into an award-winning CEO and entrepreneur.[1]

This has been an unbelievable turnaround for me. As you'll see, I was *not* someone who could have been (or should have been) trusted. I was the guy who would steal your money and then *help* you try to find it. But today, I'm a guy people trust with their careers and livelihood. Businesses trust me to help them get their startups off the ground. Employees trust me enough to uproot their families and move across the country to work with me. That's nuts—but that's the power of the Mask-Free Program I am going to teach you in this book. It's a program *anyone* can use to turn around how they live and lead. To understand it, though, you first have to understand my story. So, allow me to introduce you to Michael Brody-Waite, circa 2001.

---

1 This program is inspired by my combination of experiences in recovery from drug addiction and seventeen years of business leadership. It is meant to help anyone, non-addict and recovering addict alike, learn how to live and lead mask-free. If you are someone struggling with addiction, I want to be absolutely clear: get help immediately! This book is built around my experience in recovery, but it is in NO WAY a replacement for an actual drug and alcohol recovery program. There are tons of quality resources out there, such as twelve-step programs, rehab facilities, therapists, and detox centers. Find one. You can survive and thrive professionally using the concepts in this book—but only after you start your recovery. If you are living in the U.S., you can visit www.samhsa.org or call "211" (www.211.org) for help.

## MY DAILY WAKE AND BAKE

Alcohol. Weed. Food. More alcohol. More weed.

If I had created a budget in my early twenties, that would have been it. From the moment I woke up in the morning until whenever I passed out at night, my mission was to get and use as much alcohol and drugs as I could. Some people call this the *wake and bake*. As soon as I woke up (usually around 11:00 a.m.), I hit the weed pipe. The goal was to get high again as quickly as possible before the hangover from the previous night kicked in. All I wanted to do was get high and stay high. I was a liar and a thief. I stole from my friends and family. I told so many lies that I couldn't remember the truth. Thanks to my addiction, I was kicked out of school, forced out of my house, and fired from my job—several jobs, actually. I had no money and what I assume was a single-digit credit score. The only thing keeping me off the streets was a friend's couch. That was convenient, because the only money I had was what I stole from him during the day while he was at work. I had one pair of pants that didn't fit, and I didn't have a belt to hold them up. So, you'd find me stumbling down the streets of Los Angeles with baggy clown pants cinched up with a piece of rope. Classy, right?

At least I had my health—except for the giant beer gut. And the blood I had recently thrown up. And the fact that my lungs were so scarred from smoking that I felt like I was drowning every time I took a breath. Oh, and my liver. My doctor once told me that the only thing higher than I was were my liver enzymes. I'm no expert, but that didn't sound good. It didn't matter, though; I was pretty sure I'd be dead by thirty, anyway. And I was fine with that.

### Killing Myself Slowly

I got into drugs and alcohol in college, and I fell *hard* into that lifestyle. I quickly became addicted, and I poured poison into my system nonstop. Not surprisingly, my grades took a nosedive—along with my attitude and behavior—and I was ultimately asked to leave school. They really weren't *asking* so much as they were *kicking me out*. And where do you go when school doesn't want you and you're basically unemployable? That's right: you go to work for your parents. I somehow conned my folks into "hiring" me to digitize a lot of old papers and newsletters they'd been wanting to throw out. Here's what that "job" looked like: I got to their house late in the morning and sat down at the computer with some of the newsletters nearby. I then spent the next eight hours surfing the internet and pirating thousands of songs online. Throw in some meals from Mom and Dad's kitchen and some afternoon television, and that shaped up to a full day at the office. Because my parents weren't computer literate, it was easy to excuse the slow progress. "Digitizing all this stuff is technically challenging," I said. "It's a lot of work, but we'll get there…eventually."

Apparently, my skills as a paperwork digitizer earned me another key position with my folks: professional house sitter. My parents decided to take a long vacation and asked me to live in their house for the month. I had three responsibilities while they were gone:

1. Take care of my childhood cat.
2. Clean out the birdcages every day.
3. Shred a stack of old documents they wanted to recycle.

"No problem," I said. "I think I can manage all that." Needless to say, I didn't manage *any* of that. I spent the entire month drunk and high. Every day was pretty much the same: wake, bake, watch TV, have some food delivered, drink, eat, bake, drink, watch TV, bake, drink, eat, pass out. I don't remember many details about that month. Occasionally, I'd realize someone was mad at me or I'd lost my keys or phone, and the only way to trigger the memories about what had happened was to track my trails of vomit. After getting an angry text from a buddy one morning, for example, I found a pile of puke near the front door and remembered, *Oh yeah. He's mad at me because I kicked him out of the house for beating me at a video game last night.* You know you have a problem when you depend on day-old vomit trails for a daily journal.

The day before my parents got home from their trip, I realized I hadn't done anything they asked me to do. The birdcages had not been changed in thirty days. I hadn't touched the stack of recycling (and had no plans of doing so). I had only scooped the cat litter twice in a month. The filth from my complete lack of home hygiene (not to mention a month's worth of bird and cat poop) caused a massive gnat infestation throughout the house. I still laugh remembering myself running around the house holding a vacuum cleaner in the air trying to suck up all the gnats flying around. Newsflash: that doesn't work. The only thing of any value I'd done the entire month was keep my cat alive. There was no way I was going to let anything happen to him. The truth is, I loved that cat more than I loved myself.

During this time, I had pretty much given up on life. I endlessly watched—maybe even worshipped—movies like *Leaving Las Vegas* and *Fear and Loathing in Las Vegas*. I tried to overdose. I made ... *poor* ... relationship decisions. I drove drunk all the time. One day, I was driving down Sunset Boulevard completely wasted. A police car pulled up beside me, and my first thought was, *Good. Finally. I guess this is going to be it.* It wasn't. The cop just told me to slow down and drove off. An hour later, I took a hard turn at ninety miles per hour and almost flipped my SUV. It would have killed me for sure, but my overriding thought was, *Whatever.* I honestly didn't care if I lived or died. I basically had three options staring me in the face: die quickly in an overdose or accident, die slowly as the drugs destroyed my body, or get help. Of those three options—the first two of which involved me *dying*—it was the third that scared me most. I would rather have died than have to deal with the mess my life had become at that point.

## Addiction Is Hard Work

Movies, especially comedies, often glorify the drug and alcohol lifestyle. They make it look so fun and carefree, with the wasted goofball being the life of the party. I totally get how addiction can look to the outside world, but that's not how it is at all, at least for me. Being an active drug addict was hard work. Doing the drugs was the easy part; what was hard was having to manage every little piece of my life around my all-consuming *need* to get high and stay high. Addicts spend entire days doing whatever it takes to fund our habit, including stealing from our friends and family. Anything that didn't lead to a *buzz* was a *buzzkill*. Anything that didn't feed my addiction was the enemy. I had to figure out how to turn every interaction and opportunity into a chance to get what I wanted. And, along the way, I had to lie every minute of every day to the people around me about what I was doing and who I'd become.

> Doing the drugs was the easy part; what was hard was having to manage every little piece of my life around my all-consuming *need* to get high and stay high.

For example, I could never let anyone know that I had a problem. Whenever my family or friends started poking around the edges of that conversation, I immediately shifted into one of three defensive reactions: I laughed it off, got mad, or went into avoidance mode. As much as possible, I avoided any discussion with any person that might lead to a surprise intervention. I didn't see my parents very often because I knew they'd see straight through my bloodshot eyes. As things got really bad, even my drinking buddies got worried about me—so I stopped drinking with them. I didn't want to hear their concerns. Whenever avoidance failed and someone *did* get through my defenses and try to confront me, I relied on humor and anger to keep me "safe." They were the twin shields I used to hide how weak and broken I really was.

My only offensive weapon was lying—and I lied *a lot*. I lied about having a problem. I lied about stealing from my friends. I lied about having my drug use under control. I lied about my grades, my work, my relationships, and anything else that could have given me away. All my energy was focused on trying to look put together on the outside while I was falling apart on the inside.

I also ignored my problem by saying yes to things I had no business saying yes to—even something as stupid as a Big Mac. I'd be drunk and high at home alone, see a McDonald's commercial on TV, and think, *Man, a burger sounds really good.* Then, I'd hop in my car and make a burger run, risking my life and the lives of everyone else on the road in the process. Or, if I was completely wasted and barely conscious but someone offered me a drug I'd never tried before, I said yes. After all, it would have been rude to turn down such a generous offer. So, I just kept saying yes, even when it put myself or others in danger.

One of the hardest parts of the whole addiction lifestyle for me was the need to act like a completely different person to fit in with whomever I was with. I've always been a pretty sensitive guy with big emotions, but that seemed like the very definition of weakness for a man, at least when I was growing up. When I was a kid, the other guys at school made fun of me relentlessly for being so soft-hearted. The girls seemed to like it, but only up to a point. I was always the safe, reliable, trustworthy friend. Translation: I was the guy the girls complained to about the moronic jerks they were dating. The girls—most of whom I had crushes on—came to visit me in my little lovesick prison, safely tucked away in the friend zone, to get my advice on their love lives. My advice? *Date me!* Of course, I could never say that. It's not what I thought these girlfriends (emphasis on *friends*) wanted me to be. So, I

> **All my energy was focused on trying to look put together on the outside while I was falling apart on the inside.**

held back what I was really thinking and fed them what I thought they wanted to hear.

After barely getting through the emotional minefield that was high school, I knew "Sensitive Michael" would get eaten alive at college ...so I reinvented myself. I became the cool, distant guy who didn't seem to give a crap about anything. Getting high and drunk allowed me to cover up my emotional "weaknesses" and pretend I was strong, pretend that I was a *real* man. That seems so weird to me today, because I honestly think my emotional intelligence is one of the most valuable things about me. It's what ultimately helped me build a business and a platform to help people. In a way, it's why you're reading this book. Throughout my entire life, I had something uniquely valuable to offer the world, and I held it back out of fear. I wasted so much time and energy trying to hold back what made me *me*, and it was exhausting.

> Throughout my entire life, I had something uniquely valuable to offer the world, and I held it back out of fear.

My drug addiction didn't just make me a drug addict; it also made me a fraud. It impacted every part of my life and changed every one of my behaviors. It aligned every thought, desire, and action around a single goal: to get high and stay high. As hard as it was to get clean,[2] my life *before* recovery was ten times harder. My worst day clean was better than my best day using. It was an endless loop of lying and hiding, never giving me a chance to be real, to be me. Getting free of that, I've

---

2 People in recovery from addiction typically have a term they use to describe the length of time that they are not participating in that addiction. The most popular term is "sober." I was taught to say "clean" in my specific recovery program, so I personally use that term. If you are in recovery, no matter what you were addicted to, what program you are in, or whatever term you use to communicate your time in recovery, I respect, embrace, and love you all.

discovered, is one of the greatest gifts of recovery—but it's one most people have never really thought about.

It's time to think about it.

## LIFE IN RECOVERY

Before I get into the specifics of the program I'm going to unpack for you in this book, I need to show you how this material transformed my own life and leadership. You've already gotten a glimpse of me at my worst; now, let's look at what my life is like in recovery.

My first job out of rehab was a retail position at a local Sam Goody music store. I wasn't changing the world, but I could at least save a few people from wasting their money on Phish albums. After a while, I was ready to step up and took a sales position at a huge Fortune 50 company. I was pretty good at it, and I discovered a passion for business and leadership. I broke a few company sales records and got my leaders' attention. They made me a sales manager, and the team I led consistently outsold the other teams. It was weird looking back on the time just a couple of years earlier when I felt worthless and wanted to die. The drunk, depressed, semi-suicidal guy was gone, replaced by a bright-eyed, optimistic, award-winning professional.

By 2010, the nation was wading through a serious recession, but I was riding high on a wave of success and enthusiasm. Jobs were scarce back then, and I was blessed to have a solid position at a relatively secure company. There was only one problem: I was ready to leave. I loved my job, but I had a burning passion to do more. I wanted to build something, to create something new and powerful that would change the world. It was my life's dream to become a successful entrepreneur. I'd lost that dream to my addiction, but they taught me in recovery that my lost dreams could be reawakened.

I'd spent the last several years consuming business and leadership books with the same appetite I used to have for drugs and alcohol, and I was bursting at the seams to prove myself on my own. So, I made the tough decision to leave my "safe" position and cofound InQuicker, a healthcare software as a service (SaaS) startup. My business partner and I created a company that revolutionized how patients schedule appointments with doctors and hospitals, moving it from phone calls to a quick, convenient online scheduling and check-in system. This dramatically reduced wait times for hundreds of thousands of patients every year in hundreds of hospitals and doctor offices across thirty states. More importantly, we created a work culture and system of leadership that shot through the healthcare market like lightning. During my six years as CEO, InQuicker experienced 20,000 percent revenue growth, which earned us a spot on the Inc. 500 list of fastest-growing companies. We were named one of the "Best Places to Work" by the *Nashville Business Journal* four times and were recognized by the Nashville Chamber of Commerce as Healthcare Company of the Year. Our company, team, revenues, and national impact exploded, and in 2015, InQuicker was acquired by a publicly traded company.

> I realized that to *live* like a recovering addict meant I had to *lead* like one too.

Let's put this in perspective. At age twenty-one, I was hopelessly addicted to drugs and wanted to die. At twenty-three, I fought through recovery and started a new life with nothing more than the promise that the principles I learned in recovery would enable me to survive and thrive. At age thirty-six, I was a millionaire and an award-winning CEO. Then, at thirty-seven, I became the CEO of the Nashville Entrepreneur Center, the front door to Nashville's entrepreneurial ecosystem. In my time there, we tripled our impact from helping seven hundred entrepreneurs start or grow a business per year to helping two thousand. Today,

I'm a three-time CEO and a full-time business and leadership coach who is asked to speak to thousands of professionals every year. How in the world did this happen? How did I get here from where I started?

It's because I realized that to *live* like a recovering addict meant I had to *lead* like one too.

## THANK GOD FOR ADDICTION

I've been on a wild, strange journey through life and business for nearly two decades, and I believe—no, I *know*—there's value for you in what I've discovered. That value isn't about me, however; it's about the foundation I was given in recovery when I learned a program and set of principles that saved my life. That's why I can make the bold claim that I'm *thankful* for my drug addiction. In fact, I'm more thankful for my addiction than I am for anything else in my life. Thanks to my addiction, I was able to take everything I learned in recovery, combine it with everything I've learned as a leader, and create the program and set of principles that I will share with you in this book. What I have learned in recovery showed me how to truly live like I'd never lived before. I'm not successful today *in spite of* my addiction; I'm successful *because* of my addiction. Like a fellow addict once told me, "You know what we do in these meetings? We turn crap into fertilizer!" Lucky for me, I've had access to an enormous pile of fertilizer.

> **I'm more thankful for my addiction than I am for anything else in my life.**

Many people would assume my addiction was the worst thing ever, the thing I'd want to spend the rest of my life forgetting. No way. Sure, my addiction was the worst thing in my life for a while. But now? Now it's the best thing about me, because it gave me a competitive advantage I'll explain in chapter 3. If I had stayed the same person I was that night on Venice Beach, I would have been dead by age thirty; there's no doubt in my mind. But I didn't stay there. I got help. I entered recovery, and recovery taught me how to stop lying about who I am and what I want out of life. Recovery taught me how to be real—*really real*—for the first time. And now, I can't imagine what my life would be like today without that experience.

We've been trained our whole lives to do X, Y, and Z to get the results we want. Sadly, X, Y, and Z rarely reflect who we really are. We learn to put on a happy face, put our best foot forward, and never let

> There's a high price to pay for hiding our true selves.

'em see us sweat. But there's a high price to pay for hiding our true selves. Fortunately, there's good news. You can get all the things you want in life without paying that price. I'm going to show you how to unlock a secret superpower—the single biggest untapped competitive advantage you could ever imagine—that will make you a hero to your company, team, community, family, and friends. It's a skill anyone can master but few ever do, a skill that will unlock your true potential in a way you never thought possible. It's the skill of living mask-free.

The skill of living mask-free enabled me to flourish at all levels of leadership, from retail to corporate manager to CEO, and to build and grow award-winning teams. I've also used it outside of work to improve every other part of my life, including getting rid of $100,000 in debt, losing forty pounds, and growing into the husband and father my family deserves. In every part of my life, I've seen firsthand how much better life can be when you're bold enough to live mask-free—to be the real you no matter what. If you're reading this book, I want you to know right now that it's possible to both let your guard down *and* be a successful leader …*if* you're ready to do what I've done over the years.

My dreams were unlocked when I took the steps necessary to get clean. But, when I started, it wasn't easy and it certainly wasn't comfortable. I remember freaking out about the entire recovery process early on and nearly talking myself out of it. That's when the counselors gave me some of the best advice I've ever received: "Don't think about doing this for the rest of your life right now. Focus on doing it one day at a time. All that matters today is that you do it today." That gave me the peace I needed to take the next step—even when I wasn't sure what the next step was.

The rest of this book offers you a program that can give you the unimaginable courage to be your true self, no matter the odds. And, for this process to work, all you have to do is decide to take that next step.

But remember, you don't have to focus on *forever*.

You just have to focus on today.

# CHAPTER 2

# YOU'RE __, YOU'RE A MASK ADDICT.

WALKING INTO THE BETTY FORD CENTER WAS A SHOCK TO MY system. I could not believe I was in rehab, and I immediately saw recovery as a prison sentence. I couldn't imagine a life without using drugs, and I definitely didn't want to do any work to get clean. I was lazy and selfish and exhausted. More than anything, though, I was desperate. I decided to keep a journal through the process as a way to get my head together. My entry for the first day of rehab reads:

*I threw up blood last night. God's way of telling me I need to stop. I'm twenty-three years old. I used to be in prime shape. I used to weigh 165 pounds without a gram of fat on me. Now I'm 220 pounds without a gram of muscle. I used to be able to hold my breath under water for forty-five seconds. Now, it's like drowning every time I take a drag off a cigarette. No joke, I literally have that panicky feeling inside like I'm suffocating—right there in my friend's living room watching* American Idol. *Maybe it's* American Idol *that makes me want to die.*

*Anyway, I'm on my way to Betty Ford, and I would love to say that I'm angry. I'm not. I'm tired, man. So tired of being me. Maybe I can go be whoever Betty wants me to be and get some relief.*

I'd always thought that rehab and recovery would just be hearing people say "go to meetings and don't do drugs" over and over again, but it was so much more than that. During orientation, they taught me about addiction as a disease and spent time explaining each of the twelve steps and why they were so important. I started working the steps and spent most of my time in group therapy. *So much therapy.* For the first time, I heard other people talking about their struggles with drugs and alcohol.

> **Recovery wasn't a straitjacket; it was a life jacket.**

I realized that the junk I'd been putting in my body wasn't fueling a nonstop party; it was covering up all the fears, doubts, and shame I'd been too scared to face. Listening to other brave men and women take off their masks and find the strength to be real—*really real*—with total strangers had a huge impact on me. I came face to face for the first time with what I had become. I was a drug addict. And recovery wasn't a straitjacket; it was a life jacket. I had been drowning in drugs and misery for years, and the process I discovered in recovery was my last chance at becoming the person I always wanted to be.

When I finished rehab, I moved into a halfway house and started going to twelve-step meetings.[3] Early on, I listened as people in the group shared.[4] I'd hear others talk about their day and how they tried to practice recovery. Some shares would be like mini-TED talks; they just blew me away. I wanted to be the smartest, funniest guy in the room, so I got obsessed with delivering the *best* share. I was like a little boy on

3  Twelve-Step Meetings: Meetings for people in recovery from addiction.
4  Share: During twelve-step meetings, attendees have the opportunity to share their experiences in a group setting.

a playground trying to impress the cool kids. And in that room, Tim was the coolest guy around. Tim was always dressed in head-to-toe leather and drove Harley-Davidson motorcycles. He was what we called an *old-timer*, having been clean for fifteen years. I *needed* Tim to be impressed with my shares.

Every meeting, I ignored everyone else's shares while I tried to orchestrate the most compelling five-minute talk anyone had ever heard. There I was, surrounded by people saying things that could literally save my life, but I didn't hear a single word anyone said. I was too consumed with getting ready to share. I rolled my shares over and over in my head just waiting for my moment. I wanted to make sure I had the right hook, the right joke, the right timing. I was as obsessed with nailing a good share as I had been with getting high. And when I got it right, it *was* like getting high. People thanked me. They smiled. They nodded. They patted me on the back. And when I got the response I so desperately wanted, I'd always think the same thing: *Man, I am killing recovery.*

> I didn't want them to see my mess; I only wanted them to see the carefully crafted mask I'd been showing them for weeks.

This went on for a while until one day, I came into the meeting feeling more pain than I could hide. I felt a volcano welling up inside me, ready to explode. I couldn't figure out a way to make it sound pretty, and I wasn't in any kind of mood to wow the crowd. I just wanted to go back home, isolate myself, and go numb watching TV. But meetings weren't optional if I wanted to stay clean. So, there I was, trembling in my seat trying to hold myself together while others shared. I had spent so much time and trouble trying to impress them—to impress Tim—and I didn't want them to see how broken I was. I didn't want them to see my mess; I only wanted them to see the carefully crafted mask I'd been showing them for weeks.

That's when it happened. There was a lull as one person finished her share, and all the pain I'd been holding back suddenly exploded out of me. I started sharing. No rehearsal. No hook. No jokes. Just real . . . and very, very raw. It was the emotional equivalent of throwing up after a long night of binge drinking, like I had too much poison in my system and my body couldn't take it anymore. So, for the first time, I spewed it out onto everyone in the group.

When I finally stopped talking, a wave of embarrassment crashed over me. All the work I'd done to convince these people how awesome I was had flown out the window. Now they knew how screwed up I was. They saw my pain. They saw my hurt. They saw the real me, and it terrified me. The first chance I got, I slid out of my seat and tried to sneak out

> **They saw my pain. They saw my hurt. They saw the real me, and it terrified me.**

the back door. A few steps from the exit, I felt a heavy, leather-gloved hand on my shoulder. It was Tim. He turned me around, but I couldn't make eye contact with him. I knew I'd just made a fool of myself and was sure he was either going to make fun of me or tell me to pull myself together. Instead, he did the *last* thing I ever expected. He looked right at me and said, "Michael, I've been watching you and listening to you share in here for months. And that was your best share ever."

"What are you talking about?" I stammered. "That was my *worst* share ever. I was all over the place. I was a total mess."

Tim looked at me, smiled, and said, "That share was the first time I've seen the real you. That's what it takes to stay clean. So, keep showing us the real Michael. I want to get to know *that* guy."

That was a turning point in my recovery. It was the first time in my life someone told me I was doing the right thing by showing my true, authentic, imperfect mess. It was the first time I felt like I had permission to be *real*, and, man, it felt good.

## REALIGNING MY PRINCIPLES

Feeling like I *could* be real and other people *wanting* me to be real didn't make it any less terrifying. That kind of authenticity and vulnerability scared me to death. For most of my life, I'd been anything *but* authentic. Why? Why did I spend so many years engaging in the most self-destructive behaviors you could possibly imagine? I can boil it down to three broken, misaligned guiding principles that I'd used to drive my life off a cliff:

1. I was ashamed of who I was and wanted to hide the real me.
2. I wanted to control everything to guarantee the outcomes I wanted.
3. I wanted to avoid any discomfort or pain.

Everything I'd said or done for years had been specifically engineered to hide the real Michael Brody-Waite from the world. All those little moments when I felt like people were judging me, when I worried what other people would think, when I was scared that I wouldn't or couldn't measure up, when I was worried that I wouldn't get the thing I wanted, when I was afraid of getting hurt, I always had the same response: I just pretended to be someone else. So, learning how to be me—the *real* me, the guy I'd spent years trying to hide from everyone else—was the hardest thing I've ever done.

Holly, one of the most important people in my life and a fellow addict, says of recovery, "You don't have to change *anything*. You just have to change *everything*." She is right. To get clean and stay clean, I had to learn how to do the opposite of everything I'd been doing most of my life. By *opposite*, I don't just mean I *was once* doing drugs and now I'm *not* doing drugs. It goes a lot deeper than that. *Opposite* meant that I had to examine every part of my life to uncover the underlying principles and behaviors I used to facilitate my drug use—and then do the opposite of those things. That was no simple

31

matter, because my entire life had been designed to fulfill one goal: get high and stay high. Every thought, every decision, every action, *everything* was focused on drugs. So, getting clean wasn't simply a matter of "just saying no"; it meant changing every part of my life and making different choices in every situation. Every. Single. Situation.

> "You don't have to change *anything*. You just have to change *everything*."—Holly

It isn't easy to choose one thing when every fiber of your being is screaming at you to choose another. That's what I faced all day every day. It was a process of unlearning and retraining my most basic human instincts. Through that process, I was able to develop a way to articulate what I learned, and I have boiled it down to three principles. These principles were the difference between using and recovery, the difference between *hiding* my real self or *showing* my real self, the difference between life and death. I had to learn how to:

1. Practice rigorous authenticity.
2. Surrender the outcome.
3. Do uncomfortable work.

We'll learn more about these principles throughout the book, but for now, let's start by defining each one.

### Principle 1: Practice Rigorous Authenticity

As a drug addict, my default behavior was to become whomever I needed to be to get what I needed or wanted. I wore so many masks I ultimately couldn't recognize my own face. Throughout this book, I'll show you how leaders do the same thing. You see, as professionals, we are taught to study great leaders. We take classes, read books, and research the leadership giants. We are taught who the great leaders are and how we can become them. But we're never taught that learning to be our true selves will make us a great leader.

Authenticity means being true to your-self in word and action, which is easier said than done. Any addict or leader can have a moment of authenticity and feel good about himself. But this principle isn't just *Be Authentic*; it's *Practice Rigorous Authenticity*. That means you don't pick and choose when

> **Authenticity means being true to yourself in word and action.**

to be real. It's not about choosing authenticity when it's convenient or when it's safe. It's about being your true self in every situation no matter what.

## Principle 2: Surrender the Outcome

The second principle, *Surrender the Outcome*, means to identify and let go of the things we can't control and focus only on the things we can. This is almost impossible for addicts. When I was using, the outcome I chased all day every day was getting and staying high. I tried to manage, master, and control every variable between me and getting what I wanted. Letting go of that seemed impossible; I wasn't willing to surrender until my very life was on the line.

As hard as this was for me as an addict, it can be just as hard for leaders. As we gain more responsibility, we as leaders really *are* responsible for outcomes. We own it, so surrendering the outcome can sound pretty counterintuitive. Instead of surrendering, we spend all day turning dials and tweaking systems, trying to guarantee the results we want, attempting to control everything. But we can't, and, when faced with a situation we can't control, we try to manage percep-tion to create the *illusion* of control. We use this skill to climb the corporate ladder and get the dream job, the promotion we deserve, and the raise we want. After a long career of doing this day after day, letting it go feels unnatural. However, as I'll explain later, I don't think we can ever *truly* become successful in life until we do.

## Principle 3: Do Uncomfortable Work

The third principle, *Do Uncomfortable Work*, means taking actions that are emotionally charged and cause a feeling of slight pain or physical discomfort. It's that pit in the middle of your stomach when you have to have a difficult conversation. For the longest time as an addict, I knew I needed to get help, but the thought of attending a twelve-step meeting, sitting down, and saying, "Hi, I'm Michael, and I'm an addict" was terrifying. Every time I thought about it, huge knots would tighten up in my stomach. I avoided it for years—until my avoidance nearly killed me.

> As leaders, we know how to do *hard* work; we even know how to do *smart* work. But no one ever teaches us how to do *uncomfortable work*.

Leaders aren't strangers to avoidance either. As leaders, we know how to do *hard* work; we even know how to do *smart* work. But no one ever teaches us how to do *uncomfortable* work. How many times have you seen someone waste *eight hours* on hard work because they were avoiding *ten minutes* of uncomfortable work? Recovery—and leadership—isn't about working harder or longer. It's not about doing *more* things; it's about doing the *right* things. It's about doing that uncomfortable work we too often avoid, even though it brings the greatest results.

# BEING FAKE IN THE REAL WORLD

I got out of rehab in April 2003, quickly got a full-time job at a local music store, and finally started getting some traction in my life. I was going to work every day and going to twelve-step meetings every night. Within a year of getting clean, I moved into a full-time office job on a Fortune 50 sales team and started working my way up into several managerial roles. As I progressed in my career, I started noticing a stark contrast between what I was learning in my twelve-step meetings and what I was seeing in corporate America. The professionals around me were working hard to project strength and confidence, maintain control (or at least, the illusion of control) at all costs, and hide their weaknesses. They perpetually showed off their strengths and even faked strengths they really didn't have. It dawned on me that the people I was seeing at work every day were acting just like I'd acted as an active drug addict. They hid their true, imperfect selves just like I'd done, and they chased money, recognition, power, titles, and influence with the same intensity I had chasing drugs.

> Here I was, a recovering drug addict in corporate America working so hard to take my masks *off*...and I was surrounded by coworkers who were actively putting theirs *on*.

Here I was, a recovering drug addict in corporate America working so hard to take my masks *off*...and I was surrounded by coworkers who were actively putting theirs *on*. I saw friends wear the "I know what I am doing" mask, even though I could tell they didn't. I could see leaders wearing the "I have all the answers" mask, even though they were clueless. I worked with people who wore the "I'm living the dream" mask, even though I knew their marriages were falling apart. I slowly came to the realization that drug addicts and leaders have a lot more in common than I thought. We all learn to hide behind a mask to get what we want. The mask is the common denominator.

## Identifying Masks

Everyone—addict or non-addict, leader or non-leader—has an incentive to wear a mask, and, once I knew what to look for, I started seeing masks everywhere and not just in twelve-step circles and at work. I saw them in social media, hanging out with friends, out on dates, and even when volunteering for a nonprofit. They were pretty much anywhere human beings interacted with one another. Literally everywhere I looked, I saw people hiding behind masks because they couldn't practice rigorous authenticity, they did everything they could to control the outcomes they wanted (instead of surrendering them), and they were more focused on doing *hard* work than the more important *uncomfortable* work. I felt like my recovery had given me a unique insight into what made people tick, like I had a new superpower that enabled me to spot people's masks. I saw it everywhere, but it seemed particularly counterproductive when people allowed their masks to dictate their behaviors at work.

People wear many different masks to work, but I want to focus on the four most common ones I saw my leaders and coworkers wearing on a daily basis. These were easy to spot, because they were the same things I personally fought against every day throughout my recovery, whether I was at work or not. They were:

1. Saying yes when you could say no.
2. Hiding a weakness.
3. Avoiding difficult conversations.
4. Holding back your unique perspective.

Let me break these down a bit to help you see how these behaviors manifest in the work environment. As I do, I bet you are going to think of even more examples than the few I mention.

## Mask: Saying Yes When You Could Say No

Every organization across the country is filled with leaders who say yes when they could say no. They want others to see them as invincible champions, so they take on more and more tasks and responsibilities. You've seen this, right? These are the people who spend seven hours a day in unnecessary meetings and then work overtime every night to get their *real* work done. They say yes to a new project when they're already maxed out because they want to impress their boss or get a raise, even though that one new project could be the straw that breaks the camel's back. They're already behind schedule by 9:30 a.m., but they still say yes when someone stops at their desks and asks if they have a minute to chat. They want to please *everyone*, which means saying no to *no one*.

> **Every organization across the country is filled with leaders who say yes when they could say no.**

## Mask: Hiding a Weakness

Most people cover or hide their weaknesses. I played this game all day every day as a drug addict; I did everything I could to hide my problem from my family and friends. At work, though, I saw people who were scared to admit they didn't know how to do something. I noticed employees who went out of their way to make themselves look better than they really were. Some told their bosses they knew how to do things they didn't. Others embellished on their resumes. A few turned down training because they didn't want anyone to think they needed help learning something new. Some of these were highly paid executives with a long history with the company, but they were still too afraid or embarrassed to risk being viewed as weak. So, they put on a brave mask and did whatever they could to hide their weaknesses.

## Mask: Avoiding Difficult Conversations

In every job I've ever had, I've seen people go out of their way to avoid difficult conversations. Remember how I avoided my parents and friends when I thought they were going to confront me about my drug use? It's the same as the lengths I've seen people at work go through to avoid a hard talk. I've seen well-respected leaders literally hide in their offices because they didn't want to confront an employee about something they'd done wrong. Even in a CEO role myself, I once put off a tough performance review with a sales manager who hadn't closed a single deal in his entire nine-month tenure with my company! Addicts don't like dealing with difficult conversations. And most leaders don't either.

> The best, most innovative, and boldest ideas often come from the most unexpected people.

## Mask: Holding Back Your Unique Perspective

Perhaps the most impactful mask people wear is when they hold back their unique perspectives. That's what I was doing in college when I hid "Sensitive Michael" behind the cool, aloof, "who cares" veneer. It's also what professionals do whenever they're scared to voice a dissenting opinion in a room full of senior leaders. It's what leaders do when they choose not to rock the boat, even when they know the boat is heading in the wrong direction. Every single man, woman, and child on planet Earth has a beautiful and unique perspective, a special and wonderful way of seeing the world. The best, most innovative, and boldest ideas often come from the most unexpected people—but only if those people aren't too scared to share them.

## The Cost of Leading behind a Mask

I've seen these and similar masks throughout my addiction and career. Wherever you see them, these masks bring unnecessary pain and destruction. For addicts, they lead to jails, institutions, or death. For professionals, they lead to stress, burnout, and trapped potential. No wonder mental health is becoming such a huge topic in the workplace benefits conversation. People are becoming absolutely exhausted by being someone other than their authentic selves, and a company that provides benefits like catered lunches isn't truly addressing the problem. And this isn't just affecting a handful of workaholics; it's impacting all of us.

Things aren't much better on the home front. How much time are we wasting by saying yes to more social commitments than we really need or even want? How many of us are limiting our growth in our relationships or hobbies because we're hiding a weakness? How much richer could our relationships be if we took an honest, graceful, and bold approach to conflict? How much better would we feel about ourselves if we had the confidence to voice our opinions and reveal our unique perspectives to the world? Our masks aren't just hurting us at work; they're chipping away at every part of our lives.

**Our masks aren't just hurting us at work; they're chipping away at every part of our lives.**

Remember, though, the four masks I mentioned previously aren't the *only* masks leaders wear. These are just the four I've seen most often in my own life and through talking to other leaders and addicts. Maybe you're struggling with a different type of mask. Maybe your workplace, home, church, or social circle isn't reaching its full potential because of something I didn't mention here. Later in the book, we'll use the three principles I learned in recovery to develop an action plan to solve the mask-related challenges in your life. It's a plan for an entirely new way to live, and it all comes back to the three principles you'll see throughout this book: Practice Rigorous Authenticity, Surrender the Outcome, and Do Uncomfortable Work. If you live by these principles, it's almost impossible to stay stuck behind a mask. If you are ready to identify your masks and pull them off for good, these three principles are the best place to start.

If you want to dig in a little deeper and more fully understand which masks you are wearing, be sure to take our free assessment at www.maskfreeprogram.com. There, I'll guide you through a series of questions based on my experience coaching thousands of leaders.

**You're the only person who can determine whether you have a mask problem.**

This assessment will show you a few things about yourself you've never realized ... things other people may see in you that you can't see yourself.

In recovery, we make it really clear that only the addict himself can determine if he has an addiction problem. No one else can tell him. The same is true in identifying a mask problem. I can make guesses. The people you love can make guesses. But you're the only person who can determine whether you have a mask problem. This assessment will help you do just that.

## FOLLOW THE LEADER

Once I realized most of the professionals I worked with were wearing the same kinds of masks I wore in active addiction, I had to stop, take a good look around, and ask a simple question: *Why?* Why do we feel the need to paste a mask to our faces the moment we step through the doors of the office?

We run to our masks early in our careers because it's what we see our leaders doing. When we finally get out in the real world, whether it's fresh out of college or, for me, fresh out of rehab, it can be a little unsettling to see our leaders—the men and women we're supposed to follow and emulate—faking their way through the day. We can tell they're working their tails off trying to hide their weaknesses and that they've said yes to way too many things, leaving them and their employees overworked and overstressed. We can see them quietly questioning things in the organization while they keep a smile of false confidence glued to their faces. Society has taught them to wear a mask to get what they want. By the time we get to work and see our leaders for the first time, they're already years or decades into their careers, with masks that are well worn and several inches thick.

It's hard to show up for work every day, watch our leaders engage in mask-induced behaviors, and resist the urge to start building up masks of our own. It's a feedback loop: Leaders wear a mask and start to amass the signs of external success we all think we want, such as promotions, wealth, awards, status, and power. We look at this process and think, *Oh, I get it. In order to get these things myself, I have to try to be the person everyone expects me to be.*

The result is a masked culture, a world where everyone we see at work, online, and in our communities is stumbling around, bumping into one another mask-first. It's so common that we start to see it as normal, even if it flies in the face of who we know ourselves to be. For example, maybe you deeply value personal relationships and want to make family time a priority. But then, you go to work and slowly start taking on more and more responsibilities—things that unnecessarily eat up your precious time and energy, leaving you exhausted, spent, and mentally fried by the time you finally get back home at night. You never meant to shortchange your family or yourself. However, the pressure to be the perfect employee or to become a leader in your organization somehow overshadowed your personal values around your relationships. You look up one day and realize your children don't know you as well as they could, your marriage isn't what it used to be,

> By the time we get to work and see our leaders for the first time, they're already years or decades into their careers, with masks that are well worn and several inches thick.

and you haven't seen your best friend in months. But hey, you're in the running for another promotion! You may be silently suffering, but at least the mask you wear to work has a smile painted on it.

Leaders outside of a company context teach us to put masks on too. Take what we see on social media, for example. My wife is a stay-at-home new mom and, in that role, is the leader of our home. She is grateful to be in that position, but it also means she's relatively isolated from the rest of the world. Social media has become an outlet for her and a way to connect with people she couldn't otherwise see or talk to very often. The problem is, social media brings on an influx of new masks—especially for new moms. Whether it's trying to capture the perfect picture of your baby, people disagreeing with your parenting decisions, other parents arguing about nursing vs. bottle feeding, cloth vs. disposable diapering, or a million other "perfect mom" decisions, the competition to stand out, be cool, do everything *just right*, and make it all seem effortless is exhausting. Social media can be more cutthroat than most professional environments I've seen.

> You *can* be your authentic self and *still* be successful.

Look, there's nothing wrong with advancing your career or dressing your baby in organic, sustainable clothing. What I *am* against is the pressure to do things we don't want to do and become people we don't want to be simply because that's what the world expects of us. We face that world every day, every time we step out of our homes. So many people believe they can't be true to themselves to be successful. The reason I wrote this book is because I believe you *can* be your authentic self and *still* be successful. There *is* another way.

At the same time, I totally understand how easy it can be to reach for the masks when things get scary. I've done that too. We can make a habit out of it, enjoying how "safe" our masks make us feel and how much they help us get what we want. Bad news: that habit can and will turn into a full-blown addiction faster than you'd imagine. I'm not saying you are addicted to wearing masks. Only you can determine that. But I'll tell you, after being a leader and coaching so many, my observation is that most of us are unknowingly addicted to the masks ... just like I was addicted to the drugs. A lot of leaders I've known reach for their masks with the same desperation I once had when reaching for a fix. And, like an active addict, these men and women have been surprised to discover they're unable to pull the mask off when they get home. At some point, it just feels stuck for good.

## THE HARDEST BATTLE ANY HUMAN BEING CAN FIGHT

Okay, so we might have a mask addiction ... but I have good news. As bad as the mask culture sounds, this is an unprecedented opportunity for those of us who are bold enough to take an honest look at the masks in the mirror and pull them off for good. Think about it: if everyone is running around with a mask stuck to their faces, how big of a competitive advantage would you have by being one of the few people who isn't? Gaining a competitive advantage at work usually takes a tremendous amount of time or money such as taking classes, getting a degree, or investing in a new technology. But I'm talking about a competitive advantage that is hiding inside every single person. It is just sitting there, yours for the taking. This is your opportunity to claim a competitive advantage in work and life and reclaim a level of power you never imagined was possible.

E.E. Cummings once said, "To be nobody but yourself—in a world which is doing its best, night and day, to make you everybody else— means to fight the hardest battle which any human being can fight." Get ready. I am not only going to show you how to fight that battle; I'm going to show you how to *win* that battle. And you'll do it the same way drug addicts have won theirs. It's not going to be a kumbaya, handholding kind of thing. We are going to follow a concrete, proven program for ripping the mask off and leveraging your true self, your true face, as your secret weapon, whether you are a leader, an employee, self-employed, a stay-at-home parent, or anything else.

But here's a warning: I can give you the tools and the program, but none of that matters if you don't actually do it. Maybe one percent of people watch an inspirational talk about being "the real you" and then go off and put the principles to work. We can watch a moving video a thousand times, get pumped up, catch a vision for how great our lives could be . . . and then we step back out into a masked world and can't seem to make a real change in our lives. I know this first-hand. My TEDx Talk video—"Great Leaders Do What Drug Addicts Do"—has been viewed on YouTube over one million times as of this writing, and I've read every single comment that people have left. Do you think each of those viewers has successfully rid themselves of the masks they've been wearing? Do you think all those video views have resulted in a sweeping change across America's business landscape? No way. An eighteen-minute inspirational, educational video—including mine—can only take you so far. Once you catch the vision, you still need to learn how to implement it. Vision alone doesn't change anything; action does.

> "To be nobody but yourself—in a world which is doing its best, night and day, to make you everybody else— means to fight the hardest battle which any human being can fight."—E.E. Cummings

By recognizing that we are all potentially addicted to wearing masks, we are introducing a game-changing opportunity. We have the chance to leverage the power of a hundred-year-old recovery program that has helped countless men and women in every language and in every city of the world overcome their addictions and change their lives for the better. These people faced the worst parts of themselves, put in the hard work, and achieved a level of freedom most of us can't imagine. And take it from someone who's fought both battles—if a drug addict can get off drugs, you can take off the mask.

> If a drug addict can get off drugs, you can take off the mask.

Other leadership speakers or authors will pump you up with what's possible, but my obsession isn't the *what*; it's the *how*.

I don't want this book to just *inspire* you.

I want it to *transform* you.

But first, I need to give you the one thing everyone needs in order do uncomfortable work: the incentive.

# CHAPTER 3

# THE ADDICT'S ADVANTAGE

"So, Michael, what have you been doing for the past three years?"

I knew the question was coming, but it still hit me like a punch to the gut. I was sitting in my first job interview in years, and it was literally the most important interview of my life. Everything was riding on it. I know people often say that about job interviews, but for me, sitting in the manager's tiny office at a Sam Goody music store, everything *really was* riding on me getting that job. Without it, I would be homeless and most likely relapse. And if I relapsed...well, I knew I'd probably be dead within a year.

Coming out of rehab, I went into a halfway house to help me transition back into the world. My first day there, I had no sooner dropped my bag in my room when the house manager stuck his head in my door and told me I had to get a job ASAP or he would kick me out.

I asked, "Any job?"

"Yes, any job."

"How long do I have?"

"Five days. If you don't have a job by then, we can't let you stay."

"But I just got here!"

"I don't make the rules, kid. I just enforce them. Get a job or get out." He must have seen the panic on my face, because he softened a bit and said, "Hey man, it's not that bad. You have five business days. You can do it."

I looked up at him and asked, "What's a *business day?*"

He just smiled and said, "Good luck!" Then he was gone.

I stood there for what felt like forever. I hadn't had a job in three years, and now I had to find one in the next five days.

After unpacking my bag, I started my emergency job search. The first place I checked out was a Sam Goody music store. They had an opening for an assistant manager position, so I got an application and sat down to fill it out. Almost immediately, I realized I had a huge problem. I had a three-year gap in my work history, and I didn't think "professional drug addict" was the type of experience they were looking for. I left it blank and crossed my fingers. When I gave it back to the manager, he scheduled me for an interview at the end of the week. That gave me a few days to figure out how to answer the question I knew was coming.

That night, I called my sponsor. I said, "Chuck, I have to get this job, or I'll get kicked out of the halfway house. But they're going to ask me about the past three years. What do I say?"

Chuck, trying to be encouraging, replied, "Michael, what's the problem? Just tell them the truth."

I said, "Chuck, there's no way I can tell them I was using drugs for the past three years and just got out of rehab. They won't hire an addict and, if I don't get the job, I'll be out on the street. If I'm out on the street, I'm afraid I'll start using again."

Chuck took a breath and said, "Michael, how badly do you want to stay clean?"

I replied, "My life depends on it."

He said, "Your life doesn't depend on the job or staying at the halfway house. Your life depends on whether you can practice the principles of recovery—no matter how small or big the stakes are. This is about whether you are willing to do what it takes to stay clean, no matter what."

He was right. I *knew* he was right. But I was really hoping for a last-minute reprieve. I was looking for an excuse to put my mask back on *just one more time*. But that would short-circuit my whole recovery.

In the interview the next day, the manager and I made some small talk before he started working his way down my resume. Finally, the question came, "So, what have you been doing the past three years?" I had so much riding on my answer that I froze for a few seconds. I knew what I *needed* to say, but it was so tempting to do what I had always done and lie. Maybe I could convince him I'd been traveling with my parents or volunteering to help children in need. *Anything* but the truth.

After an awkward pause, I took a deep breath, let go of my mask, and said, "Well, I am a drug addict. I've spent the last three years in active addiction, so I didn't have a job. I recently finished rehab, I am actively working a recovery program, and I am committed to staying clean in order to change my life."

The manager studied me for a few seconds before looking back down at my resume. I assumed he was trying to figure out how to get me out of there so he could move on to the *real* job candidates. Instead, at the end of the interview, he looked me in the eye, smiled, and said, "Okay. So, when can you start?"

It was one of the most powerful moments of my life. Everything in my head told me that I couldn't get that job (or any job) by being the real me. We all have something we believe is the worst thing about us,

> Your life depends on whether you can practice the principles of recovery—no matter how small or big the stakes are.

something that we are scared to share—especially in a professional environment with everything on the line. For me, that worst thing was the shame of being an addict, and I just knew that would stop me from getting the job. Every instinct in my body screamed to put the mask back on, but I didn't. I took my sponsor's suggestion and showed that manager my true self. No mask. No lie. No safety net. And hearing those four words—*when can you start*—is the reason you are reading this book seventeen years later. That one interview started my obsession with challenging the notion that we have to wear masks out in the world, especially in the professional world.

> We all have something we believe is the worst thing about us, something that we are scared to share.

I can trace nearly every professional success I've had back to that job interview. That's when the rubber met the road, when I saw up close the full potential of this radical new way of living. If I hadn't kept my mask off then, when I was just kicking off my career, I know I never would have been able to keep it off while negotiating the multimillion-dollar acquisition of my startup fifteen years later. Without me realizing it, my drug addiction led me to my competitive advantage, a secret weapon no one else knew about. And now…it's time to let you in on the secret.

## THE ULTIMATE COMPETITIVE ADVANTAGE

People spend so much time and money focusing their efforts on things like managing their time better, getting promotions, impressing their boss, making more money, losing weight, improving their relationships, reducing stress, and every other self-improvement and work-improvement goal you can think of. They go to seminars, read books, take classes, hang on every word of industry leaders, and seek out "gurus" for guidance. Why do we devote so much energy and attention to chasing the latest and greatest fad in self-improvement and leadership development? It's because we're looking for an advantage, something that will give us an edge.

But—and you knew there was a big *but* coming—when we chase down all these new ideas, we only find a marginal advantage at best. That's because all these tactics only treat our symptoms, not our problem. You want the ultimate competitive advantage? Get to the root of the issue. At the core, most of the challenges we deal with can be traced back to the same problem: *the mask*. So, if you want to have more time for work and play, better relationships, and to take your leadership impact to the next level—then rip off that mask, throw it on the ground, and stomp it into a million pieces. That's when you reveal your real competitive advantage— your true self. It's called mask-free living, and this is how I got clean; got promotion after promotion at a Fortune 50 company; had the courage to drain my savings, max out my credit cards, and start a new business; grow that team into an unexpected powerhouse in the healthcare industry; help hundreds of other startups get up and running; coach thousands of leaders; write this book; and so much more.

> So, if you want to have more time for work and play, better relationships, and to take your leadership impact to the next level—then rip off that mask, throw it on the ground, and stomp it into a million pieces.

Sure, living mask-free leads to several other benefits, and we'll talk about them in detail. But make no mistake: being the real me, living and working without the stress and paranoia of hiding behind a mask, feeling free and empowered to speak and act authentically in every situation without worrying about the consequences…that's the secret weapon over and above everything else.

## STRANGERS IN A STRANGE LAND

The problem is, few leaders live like this. I've known men and women who have willingly taken on way too many responsibilities at work, home, church, school, and in the community. They've signed up for *everything*, but they aren't showing up 100 percent for *anything*. They aren't even showing up for themselves. So, they end up feeling stressed, tired, guilty, inadequate, and unsuccessful. But, of course, they can't let anyone see that side of themselves, right? They don't want to look weak, so they keep that smiling, can-do professional mask on 24/7—even at home. But these masks aren't working for them anymore.

### The Ghost of "Command and Control" Leadership

Why are professionals all around the world like this? Why do we feel stuck in a work culture like this? And why in the world does a drug addict have such a leg up on the suit-and-tie, clean-cut stereotype of the modern professional?

> Ninety percent of leaders across all industries and backgrounds are wearing a mask at work on a regular basis.

I have been researching this for years. I've worked with companies and people across the full spectrum, from some of the world's best and biggest companies, such as Google and Dell, progressive technology startups you probably have never heard of, and other small and midsized companies. I have assessed CEOs, executives, managers, frontline workers, entrepreneurs, free-lancers, students, stay-at-home parents, and more at varying levels of success and income across many industries around the country. And the one thing I've found in common with *all* of them is that they are all struggling with the same thing: the mask.

Out of the leaders I've assessed, how many do you think report struggling with the mask at work? Ninety percent! Yes, you read that right. Ninety percent of leaders across all industries and backgrounds are wearing a mask at work on a regular basis. This means nine out of ten leaders are doing things like: saying yes when they could say no, hiding weaknesses, avoiding difficult conversations, or holding back their unique perspectives. Most leaders wear masks at work the same way most drug addicts wear masks in active addiction. It's shocking and you'd think we would know better.

**When was the last time you saw a military general, corporate executive, or politician answer a hard question with, "I don't know"?**

But, when you step back and look at leadership over time, this actually starts to make more sense. Our leaders have been wearing masks for as long as we can remember. I mean, when was the last time you saw a military general, corporate executive, or politician answer a hard question with, "I don't know"? They don't. They can't, because we're living in a leadership model known as command and control. We see this model in the military, but, more importantly, it is the most dominant model of leadership in the professional world today.

This leadership style predates most of us and, in order for it to work, it requires people to wear a mask. In command and control leadership, top leaders do most of the thinking for the organization, and the people under them do what they are told. In order to maintain their authority, leaders in this dynamic project nothing but confidence and strength in order to make sure their orders aren't questioned. In doing so, they manage perception from behind the mask. They hold back their doubts and fears, and they hide their vulnerabilities. This approach actually made a ton of sense when the core competency of an organization was to command and control its resources on the assembly line or on the battlefield. This style of leadership worked for a long time. But it just doesn't work anymore.

Our world has completely changed in the last few decades. Technology has fundamentally altered how humans work, think, and connect. Thanks to technology, we are now connected to practically every human in the world, yet *real* connection with one another is scarcer than it's ever been. How many times have you seen people at dinner connecting with their phones instead of one another?

As technology has reshaped our world and how we connect, it has also transformed our economy. For the longest time, we have been in a *manufacturing* economy. But, thanks to technology, we are now in a *service* economy. The average worker is no longer standing in one spot on the assembly line all day sticking the same gear into the same spot on the same widget for forty hours a week in order to put a product on a shelf. Everything is different now. In a service economy, *humans* are the product. Instead of sitting on an assembly line, we grow our businesses and careers, regardless of where we are on the organizational chart, by delivering services that solve problems for other humans. In a service model, the ability to connect with people becomes ten times more valuable!

**Masked leaders create masked cultures.**

In a new world where connection with other humans is ten times more important and true connection with other humans is at an all-time low, command and control leadership doesn't help; it hurts. Leaders wear the mask because it's all they know. As a result, the people they lead wear one too. Then, when the work is done, everyone gets so used to wearing them at work that we take them home and wear them with family, friends, and, of course, online. Masked leaders create masked cultures.

Let me be clear: command and control leadership isn't inherently bad. Used in the right context, it's been an awesome way to get things done. But that context is rapidly shrinking, meaning command and control is not the best leadership model for this new world. Consumers and employees are begging for authenticity in their products, leaders, and companies, and they aren't getting it. Leaders are scrambling to check the "authenticity" box, and most of them are failing miserably and don't even know it. Command and control leadership had its day, but that day's over.

The shift to a service economy during the decline of human connection means true human connection has become more valuable than ever. And guess what isn't going to help anyone win in that world? More masks. For my fellow recovering addicts and any leader willing to live and lead mask-free, this is creating one of the greatest opportunities of our era.

## What's So Special about Addicts?

That's why drug addicts have two huge advantages. First, recovering addicts have the extreme motivation and incentive to live and work without a mask. I'd love to say I'm completely cured of my drug addiction, but that just doesn't happen. Even after more than seventeen years clean, if you sat me down in front of a pile of drugs and told me I could use as much as I wanted with absolutely no negative consequences, I'd smoke, snort, or swallow everything I could get my hands on. Am I proud of that? No. But that possibility is always out there. I am a drug addict, and I will be for the rest of my life. It's who I *am*. My behaviors around my addiction—either using drugs or practicing recovery—is what I *do*. If I ever switched from recovery to using, I'd immediately throw away the life and business I've built and most likely end up dead. My desire and commitment to never go back there again is a tremendous incentive to keep my mask off and, as strange as it sounds, that sense of urgency is an advantage non-addicts just don't have.

Second, because the disease of addiction impacts so many people in the world, there are many resources available for those seeking recovery.

An addict who's ready to get help is probably within driving distance of a treatment center, twelve-step meeting, active recovery community, and other resources. That enables addicts like me to literally surround ourselves with others who are teaching and living the principles we need to overcome our addiction. It's like our very own training facility where we practice living mask-free on a regular basis with other addicts. Non-addicts simply don't have that same option right now.

If you are an addict like me, whether it's substance abuse or anything else, whether you are in active addiction or recovery, I know how it feels to believe you aren't good enough, to believe your addiction has held you back and you will never be like "normal" people. I understand how that can dominate our thinking, but I want you to hear me when I say this: you are sitting on the opportunity to be *better* than normal. You can be special. You have no idea *how* special. You have been taught that your addiction is stigma. Well, it doesn't have to be. An addict is who you are; you can't change that. But you can choose what you *do* as an addict.

**You are sitting on the opportunity to be *better* than normal.**

That's where your special advantage kicks in. You have a unique incentive and opportunity. Your addiction almost killed you. It wanted you dead. But thanks to addiction, you can find recovery and it won't only save your life … it will turn a *stigma* into a *superpower*.

When I think of my fellow addicts, I think of the X-Men. In comic books, the X-Men are society's outcasts. They learned to hide their true identities because they were called freaks. People avoided and looked down on them. However, the X-Men didn't let that stop them from using their superpowers to make the world a better place. Same for you. Instead of seeing your addiction as a curse, you can see it as a gift. Regardless of how the people around you see your addiction, you can still show them a better way. You can be a hero but, unlike the comics, your heroic journey starts by taking your mask *off* and showing the world who you truly are.

But what about everyone else? What about the men and women who haven't been through the horrors of addiction? Good news: you can take advantage of mask-free living too. I'm going to teach you the program I created for ripping off your mask in the following three chapters. These chapters will show you how to implement a mask-free recovery program for yourself. But first, just like with a drug addict, we need to understand what our addiction to the mask is costing us.

## RECLAIMING THE COSTS OF MASKED LIVING

When I start talking about masks, vulnerability, and authenticity, I often start losing some hard-charging business leaders. In fact, I've had some of these individuals on the boards of the companies I've led. They think the notion of mask-free leadership is all about the touchy-feely stuff and has no real bearing on *actual* outcomes. They couldn't be more wrong. In this new paradigm of services and connection, the masks that leaders and their teams are wearing come at a high price. It impacts their bottom line and robs them and their teams of the three most valuable resources in leadership. I call these the 3Ts and they are:

+ Time
+ Trust
+ True Leadership

Everyone wants more *time* to be more productive in work or life. Teams need *trust* to create a work environment where people thrive and work most effectively together. And organizations need *true leadership* to set them apart from the crowd and deliver their impact on the world.

But in a masked culture, time, trust, and true leadership are in short supply. And lacking the 3Ts makes individuals, teams, companies, and communities pay a high price—a price they can't afford to pay, a price that increases every day that people hide behind the masks. And if 90 percent of leaders and their organizations are paying this price, it puts you in a unique position to reclaim that cost and use it as a competitive advantage. All it takes is the willingness to take the mask off.

## Reclaiming Our Time

Do you have plenty of time in your life? I doubt it. I bet you're busy. I'm busy. *Everybody's busy.* I've seen eight-year-olds with more things on their calendars than I have. We're in a raging epidemic of busyness today, and it seems like the problem is only getting worse.

Time is the most basic resource we have; it's at the core of everything we do. However, most of us struggle to accomplish everything we want to in a day. According to *Harvard Business Review*, time is the *scarcest* resource we have.[5] Yet, when I assessed hundreds of leaders, they reported wasting 25 percent of their time every week on their masks. Ten hours or more are going out the window every week because these leaders are saying yes when they could say no, avoiding difficult conversations, hiding their weaknesses, and holding back their unique perspectives.

**Leaders reported wasting 25 percent of their time every week on their masks.**

One of a leader's primary responsibilities is to manage resources, and yet, when it comes to time, most leaders appear to be failing. We are taking our most precious resource and literally throwing away ten hours a week—that's three months a year just trying to manage other people's perceptions! It's like we would rather fail trying to look perfect instead

5 Michael Mankins, Chris Brahm, and Greg Caimi, "Your Scarcest Resource," *Harvard Business Review*, May 2014, https://hbr.org/2014/05/your-scarcest-resource.

of win by admitting that we're not. Most leaders don't hesitate to take on more and more responsibilities in an effort to make themselves look good, but let's look at this from a different angle. Imagine you are responsible for managing a $1 million budget for your company. If you flat-out wasted $250,000 of that, you'd be fired, right? Why, then, do we think it's acceptable to waste 25 percent of an even more precious resource— our time?

Most of us can relate to this challenge. Have you ever agreed to a meeting you thought was a waste of your time? And then you found yourself in a prep meeting for that meeting? And before you knew it, you were *running* the meeting? And somehow you got stuck with the email recap and being the one who had to follow up on everyone else's action items? What was originally a *one-hour* waste of your time turned into a *five-hour* waste of your time. And that's just your time. Think of the

> We would rather fail trying to look perfect instead of win by admitting that we're not.

exponential impact a leader's mask has on the people around them. Saying yes too often isn't a matter of poor time management; it's a matter of poor leadership.

Unlike a lot of the productivity gurus out there, I don't think time management is simply a calendar problem. I think most of us filter our commitments through our masks, and the mask will always prioritize *hiding* your true self over *taking care* of your true self. So, how can you expect the mask to make the best decisions for your people or organization?

## Reclaiming Trust

It's ironic that we spend so much time trying to look perfect in a world exclusively comprised of *imperfect* people. It's as though there's something inside us that forces us to be fake when we build relationships.

Don't believe me? Then why do you think social media apps have made a fortune on camera filters that give everyone perfect skin and sparkling eyes? I've even heard of people having plastic surgery to try to look more like their favorite filters.

That may be the goal on social media, but the real world doesn't work that way. The overriding theory in command and control leadership is that we'll trust our leaders if they are strong. But, in real life, we don't build our deepest levels of trust based on our strengths and perfections. Instead, our deepest levels of trust are established in our *shared humanity*, in our vulnerability and imperfections. Nobody wants to slap on an inch of makeup or spend an hour grooming their beard just to go hang out with their best friend. That requires too much work, and our most life-giving relationships don't require that much effort.

**It's ironic that we spend so much time trying to look perfect in a world exclusively comprised of *imperfect* people.**

Everyone has a person they trust the most in this world, and it's usually *not* their boss. It's typically someone who has taken off the mask and shared their weaknesses and failures as often as their strengths and victories. We grow closer as we win *and lose* together. That's why everyone loves a redemption story. It's why the second act of every hero's story shows everything falling apart. We can't relate to an invincible Superman; we're better at relating to a bumbling Clark Kent.

In the modern world, I don't care what your role is—you're in the relationship business. Our success depends on our ability to connect and work with others, but, at the same time, we're taught to hide the very things that make us relatable. The thing that enables you to connect with others is the thing you fear showing them the most. We connect to other people through our shared humanity in every part of life *except* for work. For some reason, though, we feel like we need to hide that humanity the instant we start working.

I don't know anything that builds trust better than creating an environment where everyone feels safe to remove their masks. I recently had the chance to spend a day with a team from Google. They were discussing a big internal research project they'd just completed on what drives their highest-performing teams. The researchers interviewed 200 employees across 180 teams and asked them to rank 250 attributes.[6] Out of all the factors that drive Google's success, they discovered the number one success factor across their highest-performing teams was *psychological safety*, which I translate as *trust*. I loved it. I sat back in my chair and thought, *Man, these leaders have their priorities in the right place.* Right then, the executive sitting next to me, the person in charge of the entire division, leaned over and said, "I am obsessed with this concept, and we've taken big steps toward creating this kind of environment. But how do we take psychological safety even further?"

> We connect to other people through our shared humanity in every part of life *except* for work.

I replied, "People don't feel safe around other people wearing masks, but most of us wear them constantly. If you want to take psychological safety to the next level, teach your team—starting with your leaders—how to take their masks off, show their true human selves, flaws and all, and everyone will feel safer than they do online or in most of the real world."

> No matter who you are or what you do, your entire success is based on your ability to connect with others.

6 Julia Rozovsky, "The Five Keys to a Successful Google Team," *Re:Work*, November 17, 2015, https://rework.withgoogle.com/blog/five-keys-to-a-successful-google-team/.

She invited me to spend a half day with her leaders, teaching them the program for how to lead mask-free. By the end of the day, I saw a level of trust start to develop that would make most leaders envious. Can you guess why? She went deeper than any of her people. This executive was the *most* vulnerable person there. And they didn't lose any respect for her as a result. In fact, they loved her for it.

In a service economy, the price we pay for our masks is disconnection through lack of trust. No matter who you are or what you do, your entire success is based on your ability to connect with others—your team, customers, boss, vendors, neighbors, significant other, children, friends, and everyone else you interact with. We need to have real and meaningful connections with all these people and especially the people we lead, because trust drives effective collaboration and minimizes politics and silos. But that level of trust is usually forged through vulnerability. When we feel safe enough to share our full stories with the people around us—especially our employees—they'll eventually trust us enough to share theirs. At that point, when the whole team is connected through their ups *and* downs, their wins *and* losses, their successes *and* failures, the level of trust—and therefore teamwork—will skyrocket.

> Everyone who's ever done anything worth remembering has focused his or her unique perspectives and personal convictions on a difficult task.

## Reclaiming True Leadership

The world doesn't have enough true leadership. By *true leadership*, I'm referring to the courage to not hold back your unique perspective. Everyone has something brilliant and unique to offer the world. Everyone who's ever done anything worth remembering has focused his or her unique perspective and personal conviction on a difficult task. Abraham Lincoln could have gone with what his political party wanted him to do, but he didn't. As a result, he held the nation together and brought about the end of slavery. Pablo Picasso could have kept quiet, but he didn't. As a result, he singlehandedly reinvented art. Bill Gates, Steve Jobs, Rosa Parks, Mother Teresa, Gandhi, Winston Churchill . . . all these people have something in common: they put their own popularity at risk by being true to themselves. Their need to be *true* was greater than their need to be *liked*. And, as a result, these incredible leaders and others like them changed the world for the rest of us. That's what great leaders do.

However, we live in an era of 24/7 news cycles and international connectivity and, because of this, every move a leader makes is on the world stage, freely available for comment and critique. Our leaders can connect with their followers more than ever, but without realizing it, we have become so preoccupied with what other people think that we've gone from *leading* to *being led*.

> Instead of spending all their time worrying about how to lead other people, the truly great leaders spend their time figuring out how to lead *themselves*.

Leadership can be defined by the willingness to take an unpopular stance. When everyone else wants to hear *yes*, these men and women have the courage to plant their feet and give a resounding *no*. They aren't scared of getting kicked out of the tribe. You can't lead from the safe confines of the middle; you have to get out front and risk losing a few people who aren't prepared to follow you. But you can only do that when you have the courage to be yourself—your *true* self, not the person everyone else wants or expects you to be. When people see a strong leader going against the flow and creating change, you better believe they'll be quick to follow. That's how you put the *true* in *true leadership*. Instead of spending all their time worrying about how to lead other people, the truly great leaders spend their time figuring out how to lead *themselves*.

## The Price Is Personal

Surrendering our time, trust, and true leadership doesn't just hurt us at work; it also costs us in our personal lives. For example, when we give away all our time at work, we don't have any left for our family, friends, and hobbies. We end up burning the candle at both ends until the best parts of us just melt away. I don't want to give my family my leftovers; I want them to get my very best!

So many of us spend most of our weekday hours at work. And, when we don't have the deepest levels of trust with the people we work with, we end up feeling isolated and alone. We wear the masks to make us look better, but, in the process, nobody really knows who we are. They only know the image we're portraying. That's not a real relationship, and it certainly isn't fulfilling on a deep level. I can't tell you how many times I have been in a room full of people and felt completely alone, like at a networking event that is more like a masquerade party. Everyone is bumping into each other's mask, thinking the mask is cool but not knowing the person underneath. Whether it's at work, at home, in social circles, or even online, it can get so lonely when we wear our masks. But if we can drop the mask with just one person in that masquerade party, we can establish a level of trust that transcends work. Then, in being known, we are no longer alone.

> In being known, we are no longer alone.

And when we aren't practicing true leadership, we usually leave work feeling unfulfilled. There's always the ghost of something we wanted to say but didn't, something we wish we wouldn't have agreed to but did. We're haunted by these regrets because we keep making the same mistakes over and over again. We try to avoid the day when we'll be found out and everyone will know who we really are underneath. That's called *imposter syndrome*, and the reason so many professionals suffer from it is actually really simple: it's because we act like imposters! When we let the fear of what people think stop us from showing our true selves, we pay the high price for the thick mask of leadership. In the process of hiding who we are from the people around us, we hide who we truly are from ourselves.

Here's an idea: Say the thing that scares you. Do what no one else is doing. Chase the dream that is yours for the taking. Stop paying that high price for masked leadership. Stop trying to lead others and start leading yourself.

There have been many times in my career where I took the unpopular stance, risked being laughed at, or actually *was* laughed at. At the time, it felt so scary. But I have come to appreciate that the *greater* risk is in not becoming who I am. By leading myself, I have found more time to spend on the things that really matter. I develop relationships with vulnerability that establish a deeper level of trust. I have found the unique impact on the world only I can make. Think about it: in writing this book I am forever connecting my leadership brand to my drug addiction. Who does that? Well, I do. But it's not because I am anything special or unique. It's living mask-free that is unique. I was lucky enough to have my mask yanked off my face and forced to learn how to Practice Rigorous Authenticity, Surrender the Outcome, and Do Uncomfortable Work. It's these principles that are special, that made a life-changing difference for me, and they will do the same for you.

## The Power of a Mask-Free Culture

When leaders wear masks, they create companies and communities full of people wearing masks. The more everyone wears a mask, the more the organization pays in the 3Ts—time, trust, and true leadership. However, when leaders lead mask-free, they create a safe place for everyone else to remove their masks, and together they reclaim even more of the 3Ts.

Instead of allowing their time, trust, and true leadership to slowly leak out until the team is bone dry, they will stockpile the 3Ts, putting them in an incredible position.

I know this can and does happen because this is how I went from a part-time sales guy in a mall kiosk to a manager in one of America's biggest companies in less than two years. I beat out men and women with college degrees and a decade more experience every time a promotion opportunity came up. As a manager, I couldn't control the culture of the entire company, but I could control whether I led myself. So, I led the only way I knew how: mask-free. Because my team saw my true face, imperfections and all, they felt empowered to take their masks off too. My department stood out from the rest of the company. We were full of joy and life, we loved working together, and we crushed our sales goals. That team was an oasis in a desert of masks.

> When leaders wear masks, they create companies and communities full of people wearing masks.

Eventually, leading myself this way caused me to lead myself right out the door. I felt an entrepreneurial call to build something of my own, something brand new. That gave me the chance to build a whole company around the principles and program you'll learn over the next few chapters. We grew InQuicker, my healthcare SaaS (Software as a Service) startup, from a boot-strapped, unfunded startup with a small team of people who had no experience in healthcare into a world-class, highly sought-after, industry-leading powerhouse. No one expected us to accomplish much, but we consistently beat out our polished, professional, venture-capital-backed competitors. Here's how:

+ Our mask-free company was incredibly efficient with time. We went up against companies with twenty times the employees and $150 million in venture capital, but we still won with a smaller team and a credit card.

+ Our mask-free company established such an incredible level of trust with our employees and customers that we never lost an employee we wanted to keep and had an industry-leading 99 percent customer retention rate.

+ Our mask-free company had an abundance of true leadership that helped us detect blind spots and unlock product innovation that literally changed how healthcare is accessed across the country.

The individuals in our mask-free company enjoyed a mask-free culture in which:

+ Everyone was empowered to say no to things that they felt pressure to say yes to, whether that pressure was coming from me, their leaders, their peers, or even our customers.

+ Each person was surrounded by people who didn't avoid difficult conversations. Rather than dancing around a conversation and leaving things unsaid, people dealt with issues head on. Where some organizations would have needed seven meetings to solve a problem, we got it done in one.

+ Everyone felt safe declaring their weaknesses and asking for help when needed because they saw their leaders and peers doing the same thing every single day. With everyone being open about their weaknesses, no one had to hide who they were. They grew as individuals and in their roles and everyone felt truly known.

+ Everyone felt safe to share their unique perspectives. If you were the intern and didn't agree with executive leadership, you were encouraged to say so. You didn't have to worry about politics, hierarchy, power, or ego. As a result, instead of a select few determining the company's fate, *everyone* contributed to the success.

With an organization full of people operating at such a high level, we kept crushing our goals (and our competition) year after year. Despite the fact that no one on our team had taken a startup to $1 million in revenue—let alone $10 million—we grew 20,000 percent in less than six years and pioneered a radically different model for leadership. Did our success rate ever slow down while we addressed some missteps and realigned our priorities? Absolutely. But, with first-time founders, during a recession, and no investors, we continued to grow year after year until we were ultimately acquired—and every single employee got a piece of the payout.

> We had one advantage no one else could touch: our mask-free culture.

What was our secret? How did a team of inexperienced men and women reinvent access to healthcare against all odds? It all comes down to our one remarkable competitive advantage. We weren't the most educated, the best funded, or the most well-connected. But we had one advantage no one else could touch: our mask-free culture. Everyone at InQuicker knew how to live and lead mask-free. That's why our employees and customers loved us ... and why our competitors never stood a chance.

## GET WITH THE PROGRAM

Mask-free leadership is the ultimate competitive advantage in our modern economy. There is no doubt in my mind. And it's an advantage that's available to *anyone*, but few people are stepping up and owning this enormous opportunity. Why? It's because most leaders don't even realize they're wearing a mask. And those who do—those who feel drained by the time, trust, and true leadership they are losing every day—never had a program to help. Until now.

When I was deep in my drug addiction, I can't tell you how many times someone said, "Michael, just stop doing drugs. Just stop drinking. Just stop." *Just stop*. Man, that sounds so easy, doesn't it? Wouldn't it be great if you could just *choose* to stop your most destructive behaviors? Stop doing drugs. Stop drinking. Stop eating unhealthily. Stop buying things you don't need. Stop smoking. Stop wearing masks. It doesn't work. The whole problem is, addicts can't stop their addictions; that's why they're addicts. You can yell at an addict to stop doing whatever they are addicted to until you're blue in the face, but they won't. Addicts don't recover when you tell us what to *stop*. We only recover when you tell us what to *start* instead. That's why we have programs, steps, communities, fellowships, and other resources to work through in order to achieve this thing called recovery.

Well, leaders have an addiction too. We keep asking our leaders to stop wearing masks. We keep begging them and our companies to be authentic. We see books and articles written on the topic, yet leaders keep clinging to their masks. It's because we haven't been talking about the real problem. Leaders aren't *choosing* to wear their masks. Thanks to our history it isn't a choice anymore; it's an addiction. And the reason thought leadership on authenticity is failing is because we keep telling leaders to *stop their addiction*. That won't work. Just like the drug addict, we need to tell them what to *start* instead. If you are addicted to the masks (and most people are), then I have a program for you. It's the program that revolutionized my career, revolutionized my company's culture, and will revolutionize leadership as we know it. If you want to reclaim the 3Ts, you've got to learn the 3Ss.

> Addicts don't recover when you tell us what to *stop*. We only recover when you tell us what to *start* instead.

Over the next few chapters, I'm going to unpack the Mask-Free Program I've developed to help leaders strip off their masks for good. Inspired by my twelve-step experience, this is a program made of three parts, and we will focus on each part separately in the next three chapters. The three key parts of the Mask-Free Program are:

1. **System:** a mask-free system for taking the mask off and keeping it off.
2. **Sponsor:** a mask-free sponsor to guide you through the mask-free system by sharing his or her own experiences.
3. **Society:** a mask-free society of other men and women who are working the mask-free system with a mask-free sponsor.

I don't know about you, but I hate leadership books that get me all pumped up on *why* or *what* but never show me *how*. I can't tell you how many times I've read a book and I thought, *I am so glad you were able to do X, but how the heck do I do it?* So, my promise to you is this: My experience in recovery gave me access to a step-by-step model that has shown millions of addicts around the world *how* to quit using drugs. This book takes what I learned in my recovery from drug addiction, combines that with my experience building teams, cultures, and companies, and packages it up in a program that can equip *anyone* with what they need to take off their mask in order to live mask-free.

> I can't tell you how many times I've read a book and I thought, I am so glad you were able to do X, but how the heck do I do it?

In this chapter, I explained the advantage an addict has over the average leader. Now, over the next three chapters, I will show you how to make that advantage yours.

# CHAPTER 4

# THE MASK-FREE SYSTEM

In the previous chapter, we went through the advantage of living and leading mask-free. At this point, I might have sold you on the idea that this radical, vulnerable, authentic way of life isn't just *possible*; it's *preferable*. Or maybe you have just been waiting for someone to give you permission to rip that mask off and be the real you. Either way, I know that describing what is possible doesn't actually help. If you stop right now, put the book down, and go out there trying to live and lead mask-free, you will probably fail. And that's the problem. There are plenty of leadership experts and gurus out there talking about what being the real you as a leader can look like. But that doesn't mean much if no one shows you *how* to actually do it. That's what this chapter is all about!

A key moment when I really understood the importance of *how* came in my second year of attending regular twelve-step meetings. I met an old-timer named Archie who had been clean for thirty years. One night after a meeting, I asked him, "Why is it that 90 percent of the addicts who come to our meetings end up relapsing and only 10 percent stay clean?"

He looked me in the eye and said, "You know, Michael, this isn't a program for those who *need* it. This isn't a program for those who *want* it. It's only a program for those who *do* it."

I was taught this over and over early in my recovery. This isn't something you must learn; it's something you must do. Like my sponsor told me, "You don't need to know *why*. All you need to know is *how*." It's been one of the aspects of recovery I have come to enjoy the most. When we prioritize action over insight, we don't get lost in our head. It was true with my recovery from drugs, and it's equally true with our recovery from masks. Needing or wanting to get free from your masks won't create any kind of positive change in your life or work. If you want to drop your masks, you have to work the Mask-Free Program. This program is specifically designed to strip off your mask and empower you to stay mask-free for the rest of your life. It's a program born out of my recovery experience, but I'm not just rehashing the twelve steps into a leadership paradigm. Instead, I combined the best of what I learned in recovery and the best of what I learned as a CEO into a simple program I've used to help thousands of leaders learn to lead themselves and recover from their mask addiction. Over the next three chapters, I am going to teach you the three main parts of the Mask-Free Program. They are:

> "This isn't a program for those who need it. This isn't a program for those who want it. It's only a program for those who do it."

1. A **system** comprised of the three life-changing principles that enabled me to go from a homeless drug addict to an award-winning CEO.

2. A **sponsor** who has been through the program, became mask-free, and is willing to guide you through working the mask-free system by sharing his or her experience working it for themselves.
3. A **society** full of other mask-free leaders working the same system with a sponsor.

Before we dive in, I want to offer a caution: In all my years of recovery, it is still heartbreaking to see the addict who comes to the meeting, sees their addiction, sees the benefits of changing, learns what they need to do to live … and then walks away. Please don't be that addict. If you know you have a mask problem and want to become mask-free, take the next bold step and start working the program. Like we say in recovery, "It only works if you work it."

> "It only works if you work it."

## THE MOMENT OF TRUTH

I want to set up this chapter a little differently. I am going to teach you the system by showing the three principles in action during one of the largest business crises of my career. If there was ever a time that I was tempted to run back to my mask, this was it. It was 2010, and I'd recently left my safe job and partnered with a young software developer to start InQuicker. As I mentioned earlier, InQuicker revolutionized the healthcare patient experience by enabling patients to schedule appointments with providers online. I know this is commonplace today, but it was a daring and innovative concept back then because no one was doing it. I knew we could make a huge difference in the world, but it was still a huge risk. We had no investors and it was the tail end of the recession, so I maxed out my credit cards, emptied my savings, and drained my meager 401(k). I bet everything on InQuicker and had no backup plan if the company failed. I came on board as the minority owner and took the VP of Operations position. My partner, Dylan (not his real name), and I agreed that I could work my way into the CEO spot after I'd been there a while, grown the business, and proven myself as a leader. We thought it would take a year or two for me to get there. We were wrong.

By that November, InQuicker had signed deals with five hospitals. We'd hired a few other employees at that point, we were running low on cash, and we were looking for ways to expand faster than one hospital at a time. One of our hospitals was part of one of the largest healthcare systems in the country, so we focused our attention there. We'd been slowly working our way up the ladder from the local hospital administrators to the national leaders. If we could convince them to take our software solution nationwide, we'd go from five to fifty-five hospitals nationwide overnight. It was a *huge* bet for our company. It's no exaggeration to say InQuicker's very existence depended on this deal.

The national office kept us waiting several weeks. It looked like it wouldn't happen, but then they finally called us and dropped the bomb: they were going to put InQuicker software in all their hospitals across the country, which meant instant, exponential growth for our company. Plus, they planned to spend up to $3 million in TV commercials advertising our platform. For a tiny startup with zero marketing budget, this was an unexpected shot at national exposure (on someone else's dime)— something we hadn't even dared to imagine. That call sent our small team into a celebration frenzy. We were all laughing, crying, hugging, and high-fiving one another. I had never been that excited in my life. We didn't have much time to celebrate, though, because our team was due in Greenville, South Carolina, the next day for a sales presentation with another hospital. We piled in a car and took the party on the road.

After checking into our little motel—super cheap accommodations for a company running on fumes—I tried to get some sleep, but I was too excited. I remember laying in that bed for hours thinking about what this meant for us and imagining the TV commercials that would soon be hitting televisions from coast to coast. The whole thing was a dream come true, like something you'd see in a movie. I finally drifted off to sleep around 3:00 a.m. with visions of InQuicker being a household name in just a matter of months. Everything was perfect in that moment.

Three hours later, I woke up to the sound of someone talking on the phone. I was sharing a room with Kurt, a good friend and our Director of Operations. I shot up in bed when I heard him say, "Wait, wait. Slow down. Tell me again what happened." I hadn't been an executive for long, but even I knew that didn't sound good.

Kurt finished his call and broke the news to me. He explained that our software had suffered a major failure at one of our hospitals. It only impacted one patient, but any major failure of our software at this point could have been devastating because it could have killed the confidence that hospital had in our young company. My first and most important question was, "What hospital was it?" I was hoping and praying that it wasn't the one hospital from the national system we were about to sign a deal with. "Please tell me it wasn't *that* hospital."

It was that hospital.

According to the terms of our agreement, we were obligated to inform the customer within twenty-four hours that we'd had a failure. There was no question in my mind that we *had* to tell them. This situation was a nightmare, but I knew what we had to do. It was obvious . . . well, at least to me. My partner had an entirely different response. Since only one patient was involved and there was no evidence that any harm was done, and since it was a software issue that could be fixed with a few lines of code, Dylan—the majority owner—didn't want to tell the client. He argued, "Michael, we don't have to tell them. Nobody was hurt, the problem will be fixed in a couple of hours, and no one knows about it. There's no point in making a big deal about it. You're overreacting."

I held his objections at bay for a while, as Kurt and I worked the phones trying to line up attorneys for guidance and making sure our developers were fixing the issue. Later that morning, we stumbled through our presentation at the South Carolina hospital. As Kurt and I drove back to Nashville, we planned our response to the incident. As we went through it, the reality of what I was about to do began to set in, and it freaked me out. Was I really going to throw my business—my whole career—away on this one issue? I knew our agreement said we had to tell them, and I was committed to being real in every interaction, but my partner had a point. Besides, he was the majority owner and technically my boss. It would have been easy for me to give up, keep this from the client, and act like I didn't have a choice.

I hadn't been an entrepreneur or executive for very long, but I did have one thing going for me: I had more than eight years' experience taking everything I learned in recovery and combining it with my experience as a leader, eight years' experience living and leading mask-free that I'd boiled down to the three key principles I mentioned in chapter 2:

1. Practice Rigorous Authenticity.
2. Surrender the Outcome.
3. Do Uncomfortable Work.

I had used these principles as a leader for years, but now, the fate of our entire company was on the line.

So, what did I do? I worked the system. Let me show you how—and how you can apply this system to anything.

## PRINCIPLE 1: PRACTICE RIGOROUS AUTHENTICITY

I've used the phrase *Practice Rigorous Authenticity* several times already in the preceding chapters, but what does it really mean? The best way to understand the phrase is to define each word. I'm going to start with the most important word for each principle.

- **Authenticity** means *being true to yourself in word and action.* Don't confuse this with honesty. Honesty is *telling* the truth; authenticity is *living* the truth. Authenticity is the opposite of the mask. Authenticity means letting your true self shine through unobscured.
- **Rigorous** means *strictly applied.* So, if you add this to authenticity, you get a strict application of authenticity. Anyone can be authentic in one moment or in a safe situation. But *rigorous* authenticity means being authentic in every situation no matter the cost. Of course, that's not easy to do, and you *will* fail at times. That's okay. I do too. Everyone struggles with showing their true self 100 percent of the time. That's where the third word comes in.
- **Practice** means to *implement an idea* instead of philosophizing about it. In a world full of masks, plenty of people are talking about how great it would be if everyone was authentic. But we aren't. That's because we don't know *how* to actually implement authenticity. Practice is where the rubber meets the road, where we actually stop talking and start walking.

When you put it all together, *Practice Rigorous Authenticity* is the almost-impossible struggle to resist societal constructs and just be yourself in every situation—no matter how dumb you think you'll look. It becomes a systematic way in which you can be your true self in all situations. And, the more you do it—the more you practice this—the more you increase your skill.

I realize this may sound simple, but it's not easy. This isn't something we are usually taught in leadership or business. Growing up, most of us were taught who the great leaders are and how we can become them. We're never taught that learning to become our true self will *make* us a great leader.

> Growing up, most of us were taught who the great leaders are and how we can become them. We're never taught that learning to become our true self will make us a great leader.

Don't get me wrong. I study other leaders and incorporate their tips and tricks just like anyone else. But thanks to this principle, I am not going to get lost trying to *become* them. I am going to focus my energy on becoming who I was meant to be, the real Michael Brody-Waite. Same goes for you. I know you were put on this earth for a unique purpose and when you don't practice rigorous authenticity, when you chase becoming who other people think you should be, you miss out on the opportunity to be who you truly are, who you were meant to be. You miss out on manifesting your unique potential. You miss out on practicing how to lead yourself. That doesn't just hurt you. By hiding what makes you unique, you are depriving the world of a truly great, desperately needed leader: *you.*

## Practice Makes Permanent

People are talking a lot about authenticity these days. It's become a buzz-word. If so many people are talking and writing about it, though, why haven't we as a society become more authentic? Why are people reading about authenticity while they're living out the same old "fake it till you make it" behaviors? Why are bestselling books about authenticity still floating on top of a sea of masks? It's because of the little word *practice*. Yes, people are talking about it and there is a general belief that authenticity is needed, but no one is talking about how to actually become more authentic.

The cure for inauthenticity is not simply to "stop being inauthentic." That's like saying the cure for drug addiction is to simply "stop doing drugs." Like I said in the previous chapter, you can't just tell an addict to stop; you have to tell him what he needs to *start* instead. My life wasn't saved when I *stopped* doing drugs; it was saved when I *started* recovery. But I have to work at it every day. If I ever stop practicing my twelve-step recovery, I'll relapse. In the same way, if I ever stop practicing rigorous authenticity, my mask will start to grow back.

> The cure for inauthenticity is not simply to "stop being inauthentic." That's like saying the cure for drug addiction is to simply "stop doing drugs."

### How to Practice Rigorous Authenticity

I am going to walk you through each of the three steps to practicing rigorous authenticity. At the end of each step is a box with a question and space to write an answer. Be sure to take the time to actually *write your answers down* in the boxes as you go.

### Step 1: Identify Your Mask

As I mentioned before, the first step to practicing rigorous authenticity is to identify the masks you're wearing. Start by looking at the four masks we discussed earlier:

1. Saying yes when you could say no.
2. Hiding a weakness.
3. Avoiding difficult conversations.
4. Holding back your unique perspective.

Remember, these are not the only masks. For now, as I teach you the system, I want you to choose one of these four. Later on, I will show you how to identify additional masks.

As you identify your mask and prepare to write it down, don't worry about your answer being perfect. This process is designed to be intentionally iterative, meaning you will do it over and over again. It's about progress, not perfection. Later in the book, you will do more work to help you refine your answers, so, for now, don't overthink it and just write what comes naturally.

Now, in the following box, write down your mask.

```
My mask is:




```

## Step 2: Identify Your Fear

Now that you've identified what mask you're wearing, I want you to seriously consider *why* you're wearing it at all. What is your fear? Masks are meant to hide our faces, so ask yourself:

+ What are you hiding from?
+ What scares you so much that you run to your mask for protection?

For example, I have a problem saying yes when I could say no. When I do that, it's because I'm scared of being seen as a weak leader, of disappointing people, or of missing out on something. What about you? What are you afraid might happen if you take off the mask?

In the following box, write down your fear.

My fear is:

## Step 3: Identify the Costs

Now that you've identified the fear, let's examine what that mask is costing you. View it through the lens of the 3Ts we discussed in the previous chapter (time, trust, and true leadership), and think about the challenges and frustrations you face in your professional life.

+ What are your pain points?
+ Where do you feel a lack?
+ What frustrates you?
+ In what ways do you experience friction in your relationships?

Now, think about it again through the lens of your personal life.

+ What areas are suffering?
+ Are you stressed?
+ Do you have enough time and energy for the things that matter most?

+ Are you becoming the person you truly want to be?

We also can't forget about the long-term costs:

+ What personal or professional goals do you have that are impacted by the mask?
+ How much further would you be toward accomplishing those goals if you were mask-free?

Now let's really put things in perspective. I want you to look decades into the future. Picture yourself at the end of your life. In the book *The Top Five Regrets of the Dying*, Bronnie Ware, a hospice worker, inter-

> **We each get one life to live, and I want you to pretend yours is ending. What are you scared you will regret?**

viewed the people she cared for when they were on their deathbeds and identified their top regrets. The most common regret was, "I wish I'd had the courage to live a life true to myself, not the life others expected of me."[7] We each get one life to live, and I want you to pretend yours is ending. What are you scared you will regret? One of my biggest personal fears is that, on my deathbed, I'll wish I had said no to more things. I'm scared that I'll wish I had spent more time with my family and friends instead of having random coffee meetings. So, when you get to the end of your life and look back, what might you wish you'd done differently if it weren't for the mask?

In the following boxes, write down your professional, personal, and long-term costs.

7  Bronnie Ware, *The Top Five Regrets of the Dying: A Life Transformed by the Dearly Departing* (Hay House, 2012), 227.

My professional costs:

My personal costs:

My long-term costs:

## Is That It?

Okay, we just worked Principle 1: Practice Rigorous Authenticity. You identified your mask. You identified the fear that keeps the mask on. And you identified the professional, personal, and long-term costs.

Practicing rigorous authenticity is simple to understand but so, so hard to do. This step requires you to face some hard truths about yourself, confront your fears and the price you're paying for your masks, and hopefully create a vision for how much better your life would be without them. But— and this is a big *but*—you can't stop here. Principle 1 is designed to create clarity, not to correct the problem. That's where Principles 2 and 3 come in. Principle 1 tells you *what* you need to do. Principles 2 and 3 provide the missing ingredients in the world today. They are the principles that actually show you *how*.

> **Practicing rigorous authenticity is simple to understand but so, so hard to do.**

## PRINCIPLE 2: SURRENDER THE OUTCOME

Principle 2 is Surrender the Outcome. This should be clear, but here's how I define each word. Again, I'm starting with the most important word in the principle.

+ **Outcome** refers to the *result we want or the result we want to avoid.*
+ **Surrender** means to *let go.*

Principle 2 tells us to let go of the result in any given situation. As you can imagine, this principle feels almost impossible to most leaders. It's the thing I get more questions about than anything else.

That's understandable, because leaders are, by nature, responsible for outcomes. It's basically the job description for leadership, so letting go of those outcomes is fundamentally counterintuitive.

The primary reason we put on a mask is because we are scared things won't go the way we want. In Principle 1, we identified our fear and that fear is always linked to an outcome. For example:

- If I say no to a customer, my fear is they won't be happy. Ultimately, the outcome I want to avoid is losing the sale and failing.
- If I reveal a weakness to my boss, my fear is they won't think I am good at my job. The outcome I want to avoid is missing out on a raise or promotion or making my boss unhappy.
- If I have a difficult conversation with a coworker, my fear is that they won't like what I have to say. The outcome I want to avoid is that person no longer liking me or, even worse, not wanting to work with me anymore.
- If I represent my unique perspective in a team meeting, I am scared I will be wrong or look stupid. The outcome I want to avoid is losing their respect and potentially hurting my career.

**The primary reason we put on a mask is because we are scared things won't go the way we want.**

In all these examples, I am attached to an outcome. I'm trying to control the customer, boss, coworker, and team. I am trying to get the result I want or avoid the result I don't want. That's hard enough when you're in the middle of the team, but, when you're the leader or working on your own, there's even more at stake. The more you have at stake, the greater the attachment to the outcome. And, the greater the significance of an outcome, the greater the temptation to wear a mask.

The problem is that we all have less control over outcomes than we are willing to admit. Salespeople can't make customers buy. Employees can't make their bosses give them a promotion. You can't control how a coworker responds to a difficult conversation. You can't make your team see you the way you want. When you think about it, we all have a fairly limited level of control. This is where the masks rob us of vast amounts of energy. In all four of these examples, we're wasting a tremendous amount of energy trying to control something we *can't* actually control. As a result, we have less energy to focus on the things we *can* control.

**We waste energy trying to make sure people see us as great leaders instead of letting go of what people think and just focusing on actually doing the things great leaders do.**

Leaders are the biggest culprits. We waste energy trying to make sure people see us as great leaders instead of letting go of what people think and just focusing on actually *doing* the things great leaders do. This is the key to your competitive advantage. By learning to redirect your focus from the things you can't control and focus exclusively on the things you can control, you not only make it safer to take off your mask, but you reclaim an enormous amount of your energy that actually helps you achieve even better results.

For example, the salesperson who is scared of failing may spend a lot of energy trying to convince their boss how unfair their quota or territory is. Instead, they could be redirecting that energy to making more sales calls or improving the way they communicate with customers. The leader who is embarrassed they don't know how to use Microsoft Excel can stop spending all weekend struggling through it and instead risk looking weak by asking for help. The manager who keeps avoiding the difficult conversation and hoping their coworker will wake up one day and start acting the way they want them to act could redirect that energy and learn how to communicate and handle conflict. And finally, the leader who keeps trying to be like everyone else while still wishing there was a way to differentiate themselves could stop trying to control how their team perceives them and start doubling down on their unique perspective.

I remember a time in my sales career in corporate America where I felt like my team had been dealt a bad hand. We were dead last, and it was because we had a terrible territory. My team and I were all scared of failing and getting fired. As a result, I was wasting countless hours every week telling anyone who would listen how unfair the situation was. I kept pretending we were doing everything we could, but the truth was that we weren't. We spent most of our energy explaining how we were the victims of circumstance so our peers and boss would think we were good at our jobs. Then I decided enough was enough and started focusing only on what I could control. I redirected all my "poor me" time and politicking into coaching my team, loving them, talking to them, getting to know their personal lives, sitting in on their calls, mentoring them, and keeping their energy positive. I taught them to focus only on what they could control. Guess what? We went from last to first. It turned out we weren't failing because we were in a bad situation; we were failing because we hadn't surrendered the outcome and redirected our energy to what we *could* control, which gave us a much better outcome.

## How to Surrender the Outcome

For Principle 2, there are three steps to surrendering the outcome. I will walk you through each step, and you will answer the question in each box as we go.

### Step 1: Identify the Outcome(s)

For step one, you must start by identifying the outcome(s) you need to surrender. Think back to the masks and fears you identified in Principle 1. What is the ultimate outcome you fear? What result are you scared you *won't* get or what result are you scared you *will* get if you take the mask off and practice rigorous authenticity?

Write the outcome(s) in this box.

The outcome(s):

## Step 2: Identify What You Can't and Can Control

Once you've clearly defined the outcome(s), you can start surrendering them. Learning how to surrender is simple—but it's certainly not easy. Here's how you do it. Look at the two columns in the following box. The first column represents what you *can't* control. Here, I want you to list all the things that are outside your control. Be honest with yourself on this. Too often, we think we have a lot more power than we really have.

**The secret isn't just knowing what to *stop*; it's knowing what to *start*.**

The second column represents what you *can* control. Using some of the examples at the start of this section, you can't control how a client will react if you say no to a request, but you can make sure you present an engaging and competitive offer. You can't control how an employee reacts in a hard conversation, but you can control how prepared, firm, and gracious you are. Take a positive, proactive look at everything you *can* do and write those things down in the second column.

I *can't* control:          I *can* control:

## Step 3: Let Go of What You Can't Control

At this point, you've got two lists representing all the things you can't control and all the things you can control. Here's what I want you to do: go through each item in the CAN'T list and mentally and emotionally let them go one at a time. I know this sounds overly simplistic, but there is something so powerful about this simple act and it will allow you to reclaim an incredible amount of energy.

All that being said, I realize we can't always simply decide to stop worrying about something. If you've been spending hours, days, or weeks worried about the things on your CAN'T list, the only way to truly surrender those things is to focus that energy on something else.

Again, the secret isn't just knowing what to *stop*; it's knowing what to *start*. That's where the CAN list comes in. Take several minutes to go through each item on your CAN list. These are the things you *can* control, things you *can* make a definite, often immediate impact on. I want you to take all the energy you've been spending on the CAN'T list and refocus it on the CAN list.

When you make a conscious choice to spend your time, energy, and brainpower focused on CAN instead of CAN'T, you'll be surrendering

> **When you make a conscious choice to spend your time, energy, and brainpower focused on CAN instead of CAN'T, you'll be surrendering the outcomes you cannot control.**

the outcomes you cannot control. You'll be doing the opposite of what the masks tell you to do. You'll also become significantly more focused. That focus will introduce a level of clarity that will be hugely important as we move into Principle 3.

Will all the stress and worry disappear overnight? Probably not. I'm not saying you should outright ignore the very real stressors that leaders face every day. But you pay a steep price if you let those things fill your mind and crowd out everything else. Those things are outright stealing your time and energy. You can choose to take it back. The worries may still be there, but you can send them to the back of your mind while you focus on what you can control.

What's the alternative? Well, the alternative is to keep focusing on all the things you can't control. All those CAN'Ts will keep swirling around in your head, which can send you into a downward spiral of panic and anxiety. That's where too many people get stuck. If all you do is focus on the things you can't control, you'll never be able to take the real, tangible, difference-making actions right in front of you.

You might still be struggling to let go of the outcome despite everything I have said above. As my buddy Toby says, "Ninety-nine percent of the worst things that ever happened to me only happened in my head." If I choose to focus on those 99 percent of imaginary disasters, it will rob me of the energy I need to turn the dreams in my imagination into reality.

## PRINCIPLE 3: DO UNCOMFORTABLE WORK

When you start focusing on the actions in the preceding CAN list, you achieve a level of clarity and energy that is impossible when you're obsessing over things you can't control. When you have that new level of clarity, your uncomfortable work will reveal itself—*and* you'll have reclaimed the energy you need to do it. But what do I mean by *uncomfortable work*? Let's break it down like we've done for the other two principles:

- **Uncomfortable** means *something that causes physical discomfort*. In our context, this is the visceral fear in the pit of your stomach when you know you have to have a hard conversation, make a decision that impacts several other people, or do something you know others will question.
- **Do** means to *bring about, to put forth, to perform or execute*.
- **Work** means . . . well, if you don't know what work is, you've got bigger problems than I can help you with in this book. But for the sake of definition, work is *any kind of mental, physical, or emotional effort you do in order to achieve a result or a goal*.

Addicts know that recovery only comes through hard and gruelingly uncomfortable work. We have to undo years of damage to our relationships, careers, finances, and reputations. We must take a stand

and make the willful decision to do things we've never done before in order to become the kind of people we've never been before. The same is true for those of us who want to be mask-free leaders.

> We must take a stand and make the willful decision to do things we've never done before in order to become the kind of people we've never been before.

Think about it: we've all been taught to do *hard* or *smart* work. Hard work takes time and effort. It's your typical nose-to-the-grindstone, get-it-done, push-the-boulder-up-a-hill type work. To do smart work, we read books, do research, talk to experts, and find the best way to accomplish the goal at hand. We focus on efficiency and productivity to squeeze more work into the day. The market is flooded with books and resources on how to work smarter, faster, and harder.

I've found that most leaders don't know how to do uncomfortable work. It's completely different. It's not physical or intellectual; it's emotional. How many times have you seen someone do *eight hours* of hard work to avoid *ten minutes* of uncomfortable work? How often have you seen a leader hide in his office doing busywork all afternoon because he was trying to avoid an awkward question from a team member? How often have you been tempted to call in sick because you knew your boss wanted to have a hard conversation with you? It's a lot easier to power through hard and smart work. But uncomfortable work isn't the kind of work they teach you in corporate trainings or MBA programs.

In my seventeen years working this system, I have learned that we usually avoid uncomfortable work because we lack clarity and energy. That's where the first two principles come in. Principle 1: Practice Rigorous Authenticity achieves clarity. Principle 2: Surrender the Outcome helps us reclaim vast amounts of energy. This positions us perfectly to do Principle 3: Do Uncomfortable Work.

## How to Do Uncomfortable Work

Principle 3 has just one step. Let's walk through the step and you can fill in the box at the end.

### Step 1: Identify Your Uncomfortable Work

I said earlier that surrendering the outcome will reveal the uncomfortable work. In Principle 2, you chose to let go of the things on your CAN'T control list, so let's take a fresh look at the list of things you CAN control. This will generally point you to the uncomfortable work you may not *want* to do but the work you probably *need* to do. This is the work that will move the needle in your life, both personally and professionally.

Examples of uncomfortable work might be quitting a job, having a clear-the-air meeting with your boss, killing a product that isn't performing, telling your board of directors that you'd like to move a different direction, ending a marketing campaign that isn't performing, asking for a raise while defending your value to the organization, hiring a new position, and even firing an existing employee. It could also be less about one action and more about changing repeated actions. Here, uncomfortable work might include making time for quiet meditation in your day, saying no to busy-work, managing conflict as it arises instead of waiting for it to build up over time, reaching out to a friend or loved one every day, or setting boundaries on your work day so you have time with your kids at night before they go to sleep.

> How many times have you seen someone do *eight hours* of hard work to avoid *ten minutes* of uncomfortable work?

As you think about your uncomfortable work, it may be helpful to think about who you tend to wear your mask with the most. It could be your team, customers, partners, mentees, a significant other, friends, family, strangers, or social media. I personally struggle at times with the "avoid difficult conversations" mask. I have no problem having a difficult conversation with a stranger, but the more I care about someone, the more I avoid difficult conversations. So, all I have to do is think about the people I love, and I can usually find some uncomfortable work I need to do.

I know you might be thinking, *Sure, I'll just go ahead and tell the boss no. I'll just tell the customer we can't make the deadline. I'll just ask for that raise. I'll just break up with my boyfriend or girlfriend. I'll just quit my job. I'll just fire that guy.* All of that sounds so simple, right? Maybe as simple as it sounds to "just be yourself"?

> **There is no greater uncomfortable work in this world than living and leading mask-free.**

We are all sitting on uncomfortable work that we aren't doing, and there is no greater uncomfortable work in this world than living and leading mask-free. So, are you ready to do the work? Start by looking at the CAN items you wrote down in Principle 2, then turn them into clear actions you can take over the next twenty-eight days. Write those actionable items in the following box. Remember, don't overthink this. It doesn't need to be perfect; you just need to write down what comes to you. You will have an opportunity to refine your work later in chapter 7.

My uncomfortable work is:

The space between wanting to live without a mask and actually doing it may look a millimeter wide, but it can feel as wide as the Grand Canyon. It seems so close but feels so far away. Using these three principles together as a system is what closes that gap. It's the difference between an active drug addict who knows he shouldn't use drugs and the recovering addict who stays clean. And, in a world where 90 percent of leaders wear a mask, it's also what closes the gap between the leader living behind a mask and the leader that lives mask-free.

## HOW DOES THIS SYSTEM WORK IN REAL LIFE?

Now that you have a better understanding of the system, let's get back to the story of my work crisis and see what it looks like to work through these three principles in real life. When we left off, I'd found out that my healthcare online scheduling company had a software failure that put a fifty-hospital expansion in danger. According to the terms of our contract with the client, we had to inform them within twenty-four hours, but I was facing pressure to just fix the problem and keep my mouth shut. The contract was at risk,

> **The principles don't change just because something gets hard.**

my job was potentially at risk, our employees were at risk ... the whole company was at risk and, as a result, my entire financial future was on the line. And it all fell on the shoulders of a young, new leader who was a recovering drug addict. I just sat there thinking, *What the hell am I going to do?*

Almost on cue, my phone rang. It was an addict I was sponsoring, and he was in a crisis situation. He told me about something horrible that had just happened to him, and he was scared he would go running back to drugs to get some relief. My mind immediately switched into recovery/sponsor mode. His situation was easy for me to see. I had a better perspective on it than he did because I'd been there before and because I wasn't emotionally tied to it. I tried to calm him down and said, "Hey man, I know it's hard, and I know you're scared. But the principles don't change just because something gets hard. You know what to do."

> **My recovery didn't just teach me *what* to do; it taught me *how* to do it.**

As I heard myself give my sponsee the same advice Chuck had given me, it suddenly dawned on me that I didn't have to second-guess what I was going to do. It was like I was saying it to myself: "Michael, I know it's hard and I know you're scared. But the principles don't change just because something gets hard. You know what to do. You need to practice rigorous authenticity, surrender the outcome, and do uncomfortable work."

The business stakes didn't matter. I knew I had to use the three principles. I didn't have a choice; if I was serious about recovery, I had to keep the mask off *all the time*. Fortunately, my recovery didn't just teach me *what* to do; it taught me *how* to do it.

## Principle 1: Practice Rigorous Authenticity

I started by focusing on Principle 1. Over the years, I'd developed a quick checklist for applying this principle, so I ran through it in my head:

1. **Identify the Mask**
   I wanted to wear three different masks:
   - I wanted to avoid a difficult conversation with the customer. I dreaded having to tell them that we'd had a security incident.
   - I felt a tremendous amount of pressure to say yes when I knew I could say no. Specifically, my business partner had encouraged me *not* to tell the customer. My partner wasn't a

morally conflicted man; he was just highly logical. To him, what happened didn't constitute a need to tell them.

  • Since my partner was the majority owner, I was tempted to hold back my unique perspective. Going against his wishes would have definitely been an unpopular stance. It wouldn't just endanger the company; it could put my whole career in jeopardy.

2. **Identify the Fear**

I was terrified that if I told the customer, they would cancel the expansion and my partner would be angered by me putting our company at risk.

> Fear is what keeps most people from being authentic when everything's on the line.

3. **Identify the Costs**

I had spent so much time behind these masks as a drug addict, and I knew exactly where that road would lead me. It's a lonely place. Plus, not telling the customer would have violated our agreement and created a huge sense of guilt, stress, and fear that would have eaten me up inside. I knew I'd always be looking over my shoulder, terrified that the truth would eventually come out and I'd be found out as a fraud.

For me to practice rigorous authenticity—to be true to myself in word and action—meant that I had to tell the customer what had happened. But I was scared. I believe most of us know what being true to ourselves in word and action is. But the fear is what keeps most people from being authentic when everything's on the line. Fortunately, that's why we have Principles 2 and 3.

## Principle 2: Surrender the Outcome

Once I was clear that practicing rigorous authenticity required me to tell the customer, I started thinking about the outcomes. I wanted to avoid:

+ The customer cancelling their rollout of our software.
+ Other customers finding out and cancelling their contracts.
+ The company going broke and laying everyone off.
+ Going broke myself and possibly ending up back on the streets.

Before I knew it, I was letting the fear of those outcomes overtake me. By the time we got back home, I'd already folded the company in my mind. Anxiously, I pictured how I'd tell the employees, how long it would take for us to go through our cash reserves, how many phases it would take to lay everyone off, and how it would feel to close the doors of the business for the last time. The amount of energy I could have spent focused on those outcomes was tremendous.

**I felt the pull of the mask, calling me to come hide behind it and cover up the problem behind the mask's painted smile. But the mask held no real answers.**

It took some mental and emotional effort, but I cut those thoughts off. I'd been there many times before, seeing my life end in my imagination for one reason or another. I felt the pull of the mask, calling me to come hide behind it and cover up the problem behind the mask's painted smile. But the mask held no real answers. Instead, I knew I had to focus my time and energy on the things I *could* control and surrender the things I *couldn't*. So, I made my CAN'T and CAN lists.

I *could not* control:

+ How the customer would react and what they would do with the information we gave them.
+ The financial impact to myself and my employees if the company shut down.

+ How my business partner would react when I informed him I was telling the customer what happened.

I *could* control:

+ Whether I told the customer.
+ Whether we fixed the problem.
+ If I identified the best way to communicate an issue like this with the customer, a publicly traded company.

At that point, I let go of the things I couldn't control. It wasn't easy, but I couldn't waste time and energy worrying about all the *what ifs* that were running through my mind. If the company was going to survive, I knew I could only focus on the things that I *could* control. So, that's what I did.

## Principle 3: Do Uncomfortable Work

As I looked over my CAN list, my uncomfortable work started to reveal itself. I knew I was going to tell the customer, so I started working on an action list. Over the next twenty hours, I:

1. Informed my partner I was going to communicate our issue to the customer.
2. Found a good lawyer and got incredible counsel on the best way to communicate the issue.
3. Worked with my team to figure out exactly what happened and put processes in place to ensure it never happened again.
4. Carefully crafted the communication plan for revealing and discussing the incident with the customer.

With all that done, there was only one thing left to do: make the phone call.

Words cannot express how nervous I was sitting there as the phone rang. The pit in the middle of my stomach was swirling. My contact at the healthcare company answered and we chatted for a few minutes then I said, "Listen, I need to tell you about something that happened yesterday." I walked her through it, explaining what caused the failure and what steps we'd taken to fix it. She asked a few questions, and I couldn't get a good feel for how she was taking the news. I held my breath and prayed for a miracle.

After a few minutes, she asked, "Okay, Michael, how many patients were affected by this?"

"One," I replied quickly.

There was silence for what felt like forever. I don't even think I was breathing. Finally, she asked, "One?"

"Yes. Just one."

That's when I heard it. The laughter. This customer, the person representing the organization I'd spent the past twenty-four hours freaking out about, was actually laughing at the news. I'd pictured this conversation going a hundred different ways, but in none of those scenarios did I imagine her full-on laughing about the incident. I had no idea what was so funny.

Finally, she pulled herself together and said, "Michael, when I get a call like this, it's usually about a negative impact to twenty thousand patients, not just one. I know I have partners who have a failure that impacts one or two patients occasionally. And yes, they should tell me when that happens—but no one ever does." I was surprised to hear that and asked what that meant for our expansion deal, and she said, "We're still going forward with it. If anything, I feel more confident about working with you guys, because now I know your plan to improve your software—and, more importantly, I know I can trust you." I can't describe the relief I felt as I hung up the phone. We weren't going to be ruined after all!

Over the next eighteen months, we expanded to their fifty hospitals and, thanks to their marketing campaign, we grew from five hospitals to over a hundred. Our company was suddenly everywhere, and our product was advertised on billboards in almost twenty-five states. Just as importantly, this story became part of our company culture. Everyone on the team at the time and every single person we interviewed after heard this story. As it turned out, we didn't *kill* the company by practicing these principles; we *built* the company by practicing these principles.

But everything wasn't easy and fun after this incredibly stressful incident. Once again, I had to put these three principles to work—this time to guide me through the conversation with my partner to address our disconnect during this ordeal. I explained to him that, based on the way he responded to the crisis, I thought it was time for him to give up the CEO seat and move into the role of Chief Technology Officer. To my surprise, he agreed…but he took it a step further. He said that because of the way I responded in that situation, he felt it was time for me to take on the CEO position. And, as the new CEO of InQuicker, I made it my mission to make these three principles the foundation of our culture. Every single employee practiced them, and they became our competitive advantage.

> We didn't *kill* the company by practicing these principles; we *built* the company by practicing these principles.

So, in the end, the company and I thrived. As scared as I was to live and lead mask-free in that moment, working the system proved my fear to be a liar. Things worked out better than I could have ever imagined. Does it work this way every time? No way. There have been other times when I've worked the system and didn't get what I wanted. But that's okay. In this specific crisis and in every other key moment of my career, I've found that following the three principles is *always* the right decision—not because I always get what I want (I don't), but because it always enables me to be my true self—which is ultimately more valuable than any other outcome. Following the system saves me from running back to my mask when things get scary and I want to hide myself from the world. Being real in situations like that has proven to me that I can afford the freedom to be real in *any* situation. If, for some reason, I lost everything because of my decision to practice rigorous authenticity, surrender the outcome, and do uncomfortable work, what then? Here's the power of this way of life: *It wouldn't matter. Living and leading mask-free is the ultimate outcome.* Over time, being our true selves—despite losing battles here and there—is the ultimate win in life. On my deathbed, whether the customer expanded the contract or canceled the contract, the only thing I would regret is if I lived my life behind a mask.

## YOU CAN WORK THE SYSTEM TOO

It doesn't matter what position you have, how high up you are in an organization, or whether you're part of an organization at all—everyone struggles with the mask and the temptation to hide behind it when things get tough. You may be scared right now. Your business may be on the line. You may be facing a layoff. You may desperately want or need a raise, but you aren't sure how to bring it up with your boss. Your boss may have asked you to do something that violates your personal values. You may have an employee who isn't performing and needs to go or a great employee who's about to jump ship. A client may be threatening to move their business. As leaders, we face these issues every day. They come in all shapes and sizes, from opportunity to inconvenience to full-blown crisis. Whatever you're dealing with, I've given you a system for facing it without a mask:

> **Living and leading mask-free is the ultimate outcome. Over time, being our true selves—despite losing battles here and there—is the ultimate win in life.**

1. Practice Rigorous Authenticity.
2. Surrender the Outcome.
3. Do Uncomfortable Work.

When you practice these three principles, people will see that you're leading differently—and they'll want to follow you. In a world where everyone else is hiding behind a mask, people will see that living mask-free revolutionizes the rules of leadership. And, by living this way, you will inspire others to do the same.

So, if the system is this great, why aren't we ending the book here? It's because, as awesome as it is, the system alone won't be enough to free you from the mask. When a drug addict wants to get clean, we don't just hand them the twelve steps and wish them luck. Instead, we tell them, "You needed someone to teach you how to use drugs, so you need someone to teach you how to recover from them." The same is true with your mask addiction.

**In a world where everyone else is hiding behind a mask, people will see that living mask-free revolutionizes the rules of leadership.**

For this system to work, you need the same thing a recovering drug addict needs: you need a sponsor.

# CHAPTER 5

# THE MASK-FREE SPONSOR

THE FIRST TIME I REALLY "GOT" HOW IMPORTANT A SPONSOR COULD be in twelve-step recovery was soon after I received my one-year medallion.[8] I'd spent that entire first year super focused on my recovery and couldn't believe I had stayed clean for 365 days. I was calling my sponsor, Chuck, regularly, going to meetings all the time, and having dinner with my home group[9] every week after our Friday night meetings. It had been a hard road, but my life was finally taking off. That's when I almost drove the whole thing off a cliff.

I hadn't used for more than a year at that point, and I was a few months into my new sales job at a Fortune 50 company. As I grew more and more focused on work, I realized that I was becoming less and less focused on my twelve-step program. The further I got from the daily nightmare of my active drug use and my initial fight to get

---

8  One-year Medallion: In my twelve-step experience, we celebrate every year someone is clean with a medallion indicating the number of years clean.

9  Home Group: In my twelve-step experience, this is a twelve-step meeting that meets at the same time and place every week. While I can go to any twelve-step meeting, I call the one I attend regularly my "home group."

clean, the less I *felt* it. I wasn't as motivated by the fear of going back to actively using again, the newness of my recovery program had faded, and my job was taking up more and more of my focus. Over the course of a couple of months, I had lost nearly all my motivation to work the program. That didn't mean I was giving up recovery; it just meant that I got lazy about doing the work. I stopped calling Chuck as often, I missed a ton of meetings, and I went to dinner with my home group less often—preferring instead to isolate at home while planted in front of my television.

The last thing Chuck said to me before I stopped calling him was, "Michael, you can only stay clean on ego for so long. If you don't keep working the program, you're going to relapse." The problem was, I just didn't *feel* like working the program anymore. I told myself, *I'm not going to use. I know how to stay clean. It's okay if I don't call my sponsor and go to meetings as much as a newbie.* The longer this went on, though, the more isolated I became. I'd go several days or weeks between meetings, and I rarely called my sponsor or friends in recovery. By my eighteen-month mark, I realized I was thinking more and more about using, and it scared me. I didn't want to relapse. I didn't want to lose what I'd spent the past year and a half fighting for.

> You can only stay clean on ego for so long.

I still went to my Friday home group occasionally, and one of the nights I attended changed my whole recovery. During one of the shares that night, a fellow addict talked about her recent relapse. She explained how the relapse had begun years before she went back to using. It started slowly and subtly. The further she got from the pain of active drug use, the more the daily demands of life took more of her attention away from recovery. That led to a gradual decline in the way she worked her recovery program, which ultimately resulted in a relapse.

That share pierced my "I've got it" armor. I knew I was right where she had been, right on the edge of a bottomless cliff. After the meeting, I told Chuck that I didn't want to end up like her, but I didn't feel motivated to do the work. He said, "Well, if you don't want to get what she got, then don't do what she did."

It was like he didn't hear me. He wasn't getting my point. I said, "That's the problem. I don't *want* to do the work. I know I *should* want to, but I don't. I need to figure out why I've lost my motivation if I am going to get back to calling you more often, working the steps, and attending more meetings."

He smiled, leaned in and said, "Michael, you don't have to *want* to do the work, and you don't need to understand *why* you don't. This isn't about insight; it's about action. If you want this way of life, just [freaking] do it anyway."

Looking back, this was one of the most memorable lessons I learned. Chuck was teaching me to stop wasting my energy on *why* and instead focus on *how*. I couldn't control that the program didn't feel new and that I didn't want to do the work. I could, however, absolutely control whether I did the work anyway. I could control whether I called him, worked my steps, and went to meetings. I couldn't control how uncomfortable the work was, but I could control whether I stayed clean and lived or relapsed and died.

That moment was a huge inflection point. Up until then, I had considered myself undisciplined and lazy (most of the world agreed). What Chuck taught me was that I was lacking the clarity and energy I needed to do my uncomfortable work. I wasn't undisciplined; I was just unclear on what I could control and what I couldn't. I wasn't lazy; I just needed to reclaim vast amounts of energy by letting go of what I couldn't

> Chuck was teaching me to stop wasting my energy on *why* and instead focus on *how*.

control. I wasn't incapable of uncomfortable work; it's just no one had ever showed me *how*.

If Chuck hadn't stepped in during that crucial moment, there's a good chance I would have relapsed within six months. I realized that just learning the twelve steps wasn't enough. If I had not had an incredible sponsor, my life would have gone in a totally different direction. I dove back into meetings and into my uncomfortable work, I thrived in my career, and I even became a homeowner for the first time—something I'd dreamed about all my life but never thought I'd be able to do. Instead of spending that six months crawling back inside a bottle and pipe, I spent it accomplishing lifelong goals—goals I couldn't have achieved without another addict willing to be my guide, goals I couldn't have achieved without a sponsor.

> For addicts, our addiction lives between our ears, and that makes it impossible to spot self-deception.

Early in my recovery, everyone said that, as powerful as the twelve steps are, they alone wouldn't help me much. For addicts, our addiction lives between our ears, and that makes it impossible to spot self-deception. That's how my recovery got so far off track without me realizing it. The knowledge, facts, figures, and life-changing steps wouldn't help me stay clean if I didn't have a sponsor who was willing to guide me through working the twelve steps, share his experience living the twelve-step program, make suggestions, and point out my blind spots. The twelve steps, just like the mask-free system, are powerful, but, as Chuck showed me over and over, they aren't powerful enough to keep me clean without a sponsor to guide me through their actual implementation.

In the previous chapter, I taught you the mask-free system. Now, I am going to show you why it isn't worth a darn if you don't get a sponsor like I did.

## UNDERSTANDING SPONSORSHIP

When I got out of rehab, I needed to find a sponsor ASAP. I knew I wanted Chuck to be my sponsor the first time I heard him speak. He gave a talk entitled "Staying Clean While Living Dirty" in which he shared some of the rawest and most shockingly honest stuff I'd ever heard anyone say out loud. It was clear there was *nothing* I could say that would shock him—which made me comfortable sharing everything with him in my fight to get clean. As we worked together on my recovery for the next few years, Chuck taught me the twelve steps that saved his life and, in the process, they saved mine. Working with him as my sponsor changed my life forever. I wouldn't be who I am or where I am today if it wasn't for my relationship with him. Because of what I learned from Chuck—walking with him, talking with him, and watching him face his own struggles—I learned to master a transformative way of life that not only got me clean but equipped me to become a successful CEO.

I want to break down what a sponsor does in a typical addiction twelve-step program, and then I will show you how sponsorship works in your mask-free journey. In the meantime, though, I want you to keep a question front and center as you read the following pages. That question is: *How could this kind of sponsor help me drop my masks for good and learn a new way to live and lead?*

### The Twelve-Step Sponsor's Job

The sponsor's primary responsibility in a twelve-step context is to guide an addict through the recovery process. Specifically, sponsors:

- Guide their sponsees through the twelve steps.
- Share their experience living the twelve-step program.

+ Teach a new way to think and live by making suggestions and pointing out blind spots.[10]

A sponsor is not hierarchically higher, better, or an expert in comparison to their sponsee. They are imperfect addicts who have experience working a perfect twelve-step program. This makes the sponsorship dynamic unique to most traditional structures. Sponsors don't get anyone clean or make anyone relapse because the sponsor is never the expert. Chuck used to always tell me, "I can't take credit for your recovery, and I can't take credit if you relapse. It's your journey through the steps, and I'm just the guide."

> **"It's your journey through the steps, and I'm just the guide." —Chuck**

The twelve steps are the expert. As a result, the sponsees have to take full responsibility for their recovery. Addicts can choose to use the twelve steps and sponsor, or they can choose not to. It's up to them. They get out of the process whatever they put into it.

As for how the relationship develops over time, there is a misconception that a sponsor is an addict's end-all-be-all and his best friend for life. That's not always the case and, in many instances, not the case at all. I've had sponsors and sponsees I consider to be good friends, but I've also had those that I don't. The truth is, sponsorship is about so much more than friendship. It may sound cold, but an addict has a world of people who could be his friends; his sponsor doesn't have to be one of them. In a twelve-step program, sponsorship is focused around a single point of commonality: recovery from addiction. The foundation of the sponsor–sponsee relationship is our shared commitment to work the twelve steps together. If we become friends in the process, that's fine. If we don't, that's

10 While these are the primary sponsor responsibilities based on my own experience, I understand that they don't represent all twelve-step fellowships around the world. Other fellowships may do things slightly differently.

fine too. What matters most is that this relationship allows an addict to learn a program that will save his life.

## The Twelve-Step Sponsor's Qualifications

There's no special training for becoming a sponsor: no certifications, courses, exams, internships, or practicums. There are only three qualifications for becoming a sponsor, and nearly everyone who's working a twelve-step program qualifies. A sponsor is (1) an addict in recovery (2) who is working the twelve steps and (3) has a sponsor of his own. That's it. It's so simple and has such a loose structure that I'm amazed at how well it works. It saves millions of lives all around the world. So yes, it's simple, but I'll break it down just a bit more. A sponsor is:

1. **An Addict in Recovery:** Addiction is the ground-level requirement for sponsorship. Every sponsor is, first and foremost, a recovering addict. Because they are "just another addict," you can't expect them to have all the answers. The best they can do is share their personal experience using the twelve-step program.
2. **Working the Twelve Steps:** Addicts never fully recover. When someone completes all twelve steps, they can keep working them over and over *forever*. There's no graduation and addicts never outgrow the need for the program. I had been clean for more than a decade when I met my wife, and she was surprised to learn that I still attended meetings. I had to explain to her that this isn't a program I had to *learn*; it's a program I had to *live* ... for the rest of my life.
3. **Has a Sponsor:** Just like an addict never outgrows the need for a program, they also never outgrow the need for a sponsor. Even old-timers in the twelve-step program with over thirty years clean have sponsors. Recovery isn't a destination; it's a way of life, and a sponsor is an essential tool no matter how long an addict stays clean.

One of the most powerful things to me about the twelve-step model is that there's no hierarchy—and therefore no ego—in the process. We're all in the same boat; nobody is any better or worse than anyone else. We're all addicts working the twelve steps with a sponsor, which makes it a level playing field. In recovery, we're taught to focus on the similarities instead of the differences. As a result, we see sponsors and sponsees who have absolutely nothing in common except that they are both addicts working a twelve-step program. That leads to some pretty cool relationships that turn traditional power structures upside down. For example, it's not uncommon to see a twenty-something intern sponsoring a high-powered executive in his fifties. In the context of recovery, who the individuals are, what they do, how much they make, and where they're from just don't matter. The result is a beautiful sense of equality throughout the recovery community.

> **External success doesn't hold much weight when the only thing we have in common with someone is a drug addiction.**

Just think about that for a second. Can you think of anywhere in your life where success, status, and power don't matter? Can you think of another context where a homeless guy, a CEO, a college freshman, a stay-at-home mom, a mechanic, a pastor, and a movie star can all meet together without anyone giving a rip about anyone else's job, wealth, car, or social status? External success doesn't hold much weight when the only thing we have in common with someone is a drug addiction.

## Twelve-Step Sponsors Aren't "Special"

Since sponsors aren't experts, they can't be treated as trained counselors or therapists. By design, they aren't there to fix their sponsees; they are there to serve as a guide. If an addict needs clinical help, she has to seek it outside of recovery. A sponsor can be a great sounding board but, at the end of the day, he's just another addict. It's the twelve steps, not the sponsor, that does the real work.

I remember the first time I realized Chuck was just as flawed and broken as I was. I'd been to his house several times, spent a lot of time with him, gotten to know his amazing wife, seen how successful he was in business, and, to be honest, I'd started to idolize him a bit. He was this superstar role model to me, and I wanted the kind of life he was living. Actually, I flat-out wanted *his* life.

But then, about a year into my recovery, he and I were at a holiday party together. I watched him excessively attacking the dessert tables. He was gobbling up cookies, cakes, punch, and candy like there was no tomorrow—just like I attacked drugs back when I was using. It struck me that he was in full-blown addiction behavior, substituting sugar for the stuff he used to pump into his body.

> A sponsor can be a great sounding board but, at the end of the day, he's just another addict.

It was really disheartening and disappointing. I called him later and said, "Chuck, you were out of control on sugar last night. How can I trust you to walk me through the steps if you're so clearly letting your addictive behavior run the show?"

Chuck's tone turned serious, and he said, "Listen, Michael. I've told you before: if you put me on a pedestal, I'm going to fall right the hell off. I have an issue with sugar that I need to work through, but that doesn't mean I'm on drugs. I'm an addict just like you are. Maybe watching my struggle will help you learn ways to practice the twelve steps that I can't even see right now. Bottom line: I am just another recovering addict. My job is to guide you through the steps and share my experience living them. I do that by sharing my successes *and* challenges with you equally. I told you never to put me on a pedestal, and now you know why."

That stung, but he was right. I had unknowingly promoted Chuck from my guide in recovery to my hero. But that wasn't fair to him because that's not what a sponsor is. He was just another addict with more experience working the twelve steps. Chuck was doing his best to live the twelve-step program with the help of his sponsor—just like I was.

This is just a glimpse of what sponsorship looks like based on my experience in the world of drug and alcohol recovery. There's a lot more I could say about this unique relationship and how it's been so transformative in my life, but this book isn't a primer on recovery; it's a book for teaching people how to drop their masks by practicing rigorous authenticity, surrendering the outcome, and doing uncomfortable work. So, the big question is, how does the sponsorship model help leaders do this? How can we apply what I know about sponsorship in a professional context in a way that makes sense?

## IN A WORLD ADDICTED TO MASKS, EVERYONE NEEDS A SPONSOR

The three principles we learned in the previous chapter—practice rigorous authenticity, surrender the outcome, and do uncomfortable work—form the mask-free system, but it can only take you so far. It's a powerful system for kicking your addiction to masks, but, like Chuck told me years ago, I could only stay clean on ego for so long. Same for you. If you try to work the system alone, you'll be just as vulnerable as I was on the road to relapse and you won't even know it. It took my sponsor identifying my blind spot, challenging my thought process, and making the suggestions based on his experience to get me back on track. If an addict wants to get clean and stay clean from drugs and alcohol, he needs a sponsor. And, if you want to keep the mask off and show your true face, well, you need a sponsor for that too.

> If you try to work the system alone, you'll be just as vulnerable as I was on the road to relapse and you won't even know it.

## You Need a Sponsor

From the moment we enter the world, we're surrounded by people who are teaching us how to live and interact with others. Our parents teach us their values, and we take them as our own. Later, our friends, classmates, boyfriends, and girlfriends teach us how to survive socially and navigate through a whole new world of social complexity. Then, we go to work and our bosses and coworkers teach us how to act in order to get the promotion, income, and recognition we desire. The underlying message through all of this is, "Who do I need to be in order to get the thing that I want?" We may not realize it, but we spend our whole lives learning how to wear masks because we spend all day surrounded by other people's masks.

**If someone taught you how to wear the mask, then you need someone to teach you how to take it off.**

If someone taught you how to wear the mask, then you need someone to teach you how to take it off. In twelve-step recovery, addicts can't simply *read* the twelve steps and use that head knowledge to get clean without a sponsor to guide them through the process. In the same way, you can't just read this book and recover from your mask. You need a sponsor to guide you through the system, teach you by sharing his or her experience, identify your blind spots, and challenge your thinking in order to teach you an entirely new way to live. As I've said several times, you can't spot self-deception. That means you can't see your own masks. Your mirrors are broken. You need someone in your life who you trust to tell you what you really look like and how to be your true self in work and life.

This was such an important part of my recovery. When I asked Chuck to sponsor me, I was asking him to challenge the heck out of my thinking, point out all my blind spots, and help me find a new way to live. It didn't come naturally. I hated it at first, but I learned to crave it because it saved my life and made me into the man I am today. As a result of this experience, I have a characteristic as a CEO that is pretty rare: I yearn for the people I work with to challenge me. I am desperate for them to call out my blind spots in a way most CEOs are not. I got so used to this saving my life that I figured it would help me be a better leader and help us be a better organization. It became such a huge key to my success that I now train new employees by telling them I will never fire them for challenging me, but I *will* fire them if they don't.

> **If we as leaders don't empower the people around us to help us see our biggest flaws, how can we ever overcome them?**

The sad thing is most leaders don't respond well to being challenged. They think they should have all the answers, and it erodes their authority if they don't. They think it makes them look weak. It's so self-centered and backwards. If we as leaders don't empower the people around us to help us see our biggest flaws, how can we ever overcome them? How much do we and the organization suffer as a result?

It's quite an adjustment to walk around in your professional life yearning to have your teammates point out your blind spots and weaknesses. And it's that adjustment that makes having a sponsor we trust so important. If every leader in this world had their own Chuck, we would be living in a vastly different world.

## The Mask-Free Sponsor's Job and Qualifications

Mask-free sponsorship is similar to twelve-step sponsorship but obviously has a different focus and context. The qualifications, however, are the same. A mask-free sponsor is a person who:

1. Has a desire to live and lead mask-free,
2. Is working the mask-free system, and
3. Has a sponsor of his own.

I'm often asked, "Just how much experience does the sponsor need to have?" The answer varies in both the twelve-step program and the Mask-Free Program, but I know when I was coming up in recovery the minimum the sponsor had to be was just one step ahead. The same is conceptually true for the mask-free sponsor. He just needs to be slightly ahead of you in the process of working the system. So, if your sponsor is only a month or two further along than you, that's okay. We'll talk more about when someone is ready to become a sponsor in chapter 7.

What does the mask-free sponsor do? A sponsor in this context:

1. Guides their sponsees through the mask-free system.
2. Shares their experience living the Mask-Free Program.
3. Teaches a new way to think and live by making suggestions and pointing out blind spots.

Unlike the business world, mask-free recovery has no additional prestige or power based on someone's role or title. Remember how, in twelve-step recovery, we talked about an intern sponsoring the executive? Same here. It's just two people working the system together.

## Mask-Free Sponsors Aren't "Special"

Business leaders pretend they are superheroes, and we can end up believing them. Conversely, a good mask-free sponsor doesn't pretend their way is special, and they don't try to make up their own flavor of the Mask-Free Program. The only thing that is special about the sponsor is their experience working the mask-free system.

Remember what Chuck told me: "If you put me on a pedestal, I'll fall right the hell off." Make no mistake, your mask-free sponsor won't be perfect at living mask-free. He or she is just someone who is working the mask-free system. When they fall down, or when you fall down, you will be able to work through how to apply the system together.

One of the most important differences between the traditional business world and the mask-free sponsor is that sponsors do not teach from a place of expertise or power. They teach from a place of experience—period. A good sponsor doesn't tell you definitively what to do in a situation; they can only share relevant experiences of how they faced a similar issue and applied the system, and then they can make a suggestion based on that experience. By not exerting any power or position and not telling the sponsee what to do, the sponsor actually teaches the sponsee, a fellow mask addict—how to learn from that experience and take action for their self. *Truly great sponsors don't lead you. They teach you how to lead yourself.*

> **Truly great sponsors don't lead you. They teach you how to lead yourself.**

## Mask-Free Sponsors Unlock the 3 Ts

Mask-free sponsors help their sponsees grow the 3 Ts—time, trust, and true leadership—in a significant way. But you will notice again that the way they teach isn't actually hands-on instruction or through expertise. Instead, they share their experience practicing the system. For example:

1. **Time:** Sponsors share their experience, both successes and failures, using the system in situations where they feel pressure to say yes when they could say no or in situations where they want to avoid having difficult conversations.
2. **Trust:** Sponsors share their experience, both successes and failures, not hiding their weaknesses and using the system to develop those weaknesses into strengths.
3. **True Leadership:** Sponsors share their experience, both successes and failures, taking an unpopular stance and sharing their unique perspectives. They share their experience using the system to lead themselves and in turn their sponsees do the same.

By practicing the system and sharing their experience with their sponsees, mask-free sponsors not only help their sponsees own and develop the 3Ts in their lives, but, in the process, the sponsors are in an even better position to realize the full power of the 3Ts in theirs.

### Mask-Free Sponsors Lead Themselves

Perhaps the most revolutionary point that I want to double down on is that mask-free sponsors do not lead with strengths and success like traditional leaders. They do the opposite; they lead with their vulnerabilities and mistakes, just like Chuck demonstrated when he was struggling with sugar. This is how they connect, normalize, educate, and inspire. Many business leaders do the opposite. The average leader learns (directly or indirectly) to hide his weaknesses and put on a mask of confidence and competence—even when he doesn't know what he's doing. Even old-timers in twelve-step recovery face this pressure. They can start to feel reluctant to share their problems in meetings because they think they should have it all figured out. Even though I have been clean for more than seventeen years, it can be oddly intimidating to tell a group of addicts in early recovery that I am still struggling with something. When we don't share those weaknesses, vulnerabilities, and failures—no matter how long we've been clean—we are headed down the road to relapse.

> Mask-free sponsors do not lead with strengths and success like traditional leaders.

I felt this pressure just after my daughter was born. I'd been clean for more than sixteen years at that point, and I'd already been a three-time CEO. But there I was one night in a twelve-step meeting, feeling scared to tell my home group that I felt like a terrible husband and father. I knew I *loved* my newborn daughter, but I wasn't sure yet if I *liked* her. I didn't feel as connected to her as I thought I should. My wife and daughter had this special bond, and I felt like a reluctant tourist father on the outside of his family looking in, secretly wondering if I could rise to the occasion. I felt guilty about second-guessing fatherhood while my wife was going through the hell of sleep deprivation and nursing every two hours, so I silently suffered those first few months. It ended up putting distance between my wife and me, which only compounded my little pity party. I was really struggling, but I felt weak sharing that in a room where I was supposed to be one of the "leaders." Fortunately, I had practiced sharing things that would make me look "weak" for sixteen years, so I spilled my guts.

Too many old-timers think they need to act a certain way once they have time in a twelve-step program instead of doing the very thing that got them that time in the first place. That is a recipe for relapse, and that wasn't going to be me. So, I did the uncomfortable work, shared my struggle, and, in return, received a tremendous amount of experience, strength, and hope.

**If every leader in this world *had* a mask-free sponsor and every leader *was* a mask-free sponsor, we would be living in a mask-free world.**

Allowing intimidation or embarrassment to shut you up when you're struggling stops you from leading yourself and it robs the people around you of the opportunity to learn from your mistakes. It also indirectly teaches them that *they* should keep quiet about their weaknesses and struggles too. As a sponsor, if you take the mask off and share your vulnerabilities, you show others how to lead themselves because you are leading *yourself* by facing your weaknesses head on. By sharing my struggle as a new father that night in my home group, I didn't lose the respect of the people around me; I gained their respect because many of the parents in the group had silently struggled with the same stuff. I not only got the support and encouragement I needed, but I gave my friends who were parents an opportunity to share their vulnerabilities as well. It was a win-win, but it wasn't because I did anything that noteworthy. It was because I had sixteen years of proof that this way of life worked.

If every leader in this world *had* a mask-free sponsor and every leader *was* a mask-free sponsor, we would be living in a mask-free world.

## MASK-FREE SPONSORSHIP IN ACTION

Whether you work in a company, on your own, or at home, what would happen if you sponsored a few people like this and encouraged each one to pay it forward by sponsoring others? Whether it is inside an organization, a team, a community, or a family, it would create a snowball effect with enormous momentum. And what if you were the one who got the ball rolling? You'd be responsible for transforming your entire sphere of influence, and it wouldn't be because you were the perfect leader; it would be because you were an imperfect leader practicing and teaching a perfect system. You'd be allowing yourself to be "just another mask addict," showing your people that you're just as human and flawed as they are. That would take the pressure off you having to pretend to be Superman or Superwoman, and it would prevent you from trying to create an army of fake Superman clones. When I first met Chuck, he wasn't interested in turning me into a second-rate Chuck. His goal was to help me become the best Michael I could be. In the same way, the world already has one of you. What the world needs now is everyone becoming the best version of themselves.

> What the world needs now is everyone becoming the best version of themselves.

Whether you lead a company with 100,000 employees, are an individual contributor, or a stay-at-home parent, sponsorship will help you learn to live and lead mask-free. I'll go into more detail on how to implement sponsorship as part of this entire program later. For now, though, I want to hit the high points of how sponsorship progresses over time.

### Step One: Get a Sponsor

You need to start by getting a sponsor for yourself. As we've said before, *every* addict needs a sponsor. That includes you. If you have people in your company, community, or family who are working the Mask-Free Program, then you can ask one of them to be your sponsor. But if you are the first person in your world to start working the Mask-Free Program, know that you are not alone. You can find a sponsor at www.maskfreeprogram.com.

> Masks are everywhere, from board rooms to classrooms to living rooms.

### Step Two: Work the System

If you want to be free of your masks, you have to start practicing the three principles of the system for yourself. This means you Practice Rigorous Authenticity, Surrender the Outcome, and Do Uncomfortable Work using the step-by-step method outlined in chapter 4, and you ask your sponsor questions about their experience along the way. In chapter 7, we will show you specifically how to do this with your sponsor over time. There are also resources available at www.maskfreeprogram.com.

### Step Three: Become a Sponsor

Once you've got a sponsor for yourself and you've committed to working the system in your own life, you will be ready to start sponsoring others. In my ideal world, entire companies would do this. I envision a CEO sponsoring their executives, those executives sponsoring their managers, those managers sponsoring their team leaders, and so on all the way down the line. Imagine the power of a mask-free culture!

Masks are everywhere, from board rooms to classrooms to living rooms. I've worked with a lot of self-employed leaders, remote employees, and solo startups, and they all talk about the pressure they feel to "keep up appearances" in the business community by looking successful regardless of how their businesses are doing. The same thing happens outside of a professional environment. When my wife transitioned from working full time to staying at home with our daughter, she felt pressure to wear the "perfect mother" mask with her mom groups, online communities, social media, friends, and even our family. She and other hardworking parents need support too. Try to keep your eyes open to the people around you who are struggling with their masks and share this information with them. You could be one small, vulnerable, coffee-shop conversation away from helping someone transform their life! And, of course, if you just can't find anyone to sponsor, join us at www.maskfreeprogram.com where we connect sponsors with sponsees through our Mask-Free Program.

> The moment you stop giving this way of life away is the moment you start to lose it.

## Give It to Keep It

I would love to tell you that sponsoring others is just about paying it forward and being of service. Obviously, if no one had agreed to sponsor us, we wouldn't be able to become a sponsor ourselves. So, the "pay it forward" mindset is absolutely one of the reasons to become a sponsor.

But what is often overlooked and equally important is that you become a sponsor for a selfish reason as well. We give it so we can keep it. It's highly unlikely that you can stay mask-free without being a sponsor because when you give the system to others through sponsorship, your sponsees end up serving as mirrors in the same way your sponsor has. As a result, seeing the mask on a sponsee's face allows you to see the mask on your own. Helping them work the system in their life reminds you to work it in yours. It's a two-way street and the moment you stop giving this way of life away is the moment you start to lose it. You give it…to keep it. Get it? Got it? Good.

## LEADING WITH VULNERABILITY IS LEADING WITH STRENGTH

I've led with this mindset my entire career and, as we covered earlier, it gave me and my company the *addict's advantage*. A mask-free culture allowed us to scale our talent faster, have more effective communication, more accurate information, and flat-out execute better than our competition. Despite outsized success for a team much smaller than its competitors, other leaders would think I was either being naïve or downright stupid when I described some of the "mask-free moments" I had with my team. Some even laughed.

> While they were studying the great leaders in history that could admit no fault, I was being taught by my sponsor to view him as "just another addict."

As I heard their feedback, directly or indirectly, there were many times when I doubted my approach. The more success we had, the more I heard these rumblings. The more I heard the rumblings, the more I feared this new way of leadership was reckless. But, the more "reckless" we were, the more successful we were. Over time, I learned, thanks to the perspective of some great friends, that these other leaders were threatened. My untraditional approach was challenging the "CEO Hero Paradigm," and not only did they not know how to experience vulnerability, they especially didn't know how to experience it as a superpower. That made sense. While they were studying the great leaders in history that could admit no fault, I was being taught by my sponsor to view him as "just another addict."

So, here's the deal: I'm going to prepare you for the inevitable. Some traditional leaders are going to think this way of leadership is *soft*. That it's *new-age* stuff.

It's not. It's *next-level* stuff.

For me, it was about having the strength to show my team my real and imperfect face and create a culture in which they could show me theirs. Leading myself made me even better at leading my team, and mask-free leadership helped our company scale in ways most traditional leaders would rather ridicule than replicate.

For example, I'll never forget the moment I told my team that I was in over my head as CEO. I'd been CEO for three months at that point, and InQuicker was getting a ton of exposure through our relationship with the healthcare network I mentioned in the previous chapter. We had gone from a small, unknown startup to a fast-growing company with national advertising in a matter of months, and it freaked me out. As everything started to grow, I felt more and more unequipped to handle it. I was supposed to be the CEO, the bigshot leader with all the answers, but I felt like I didn't have a clue what I was doing.

At first, I kept my mouth shut and didn't tell my team how much I was struggling, but it was silently killing me. One night during this season, I was in a twelve-step meeting and opened up to a friend. I said, "Man, how did I even get clean? Getting clean is the hardest thing I've ever done. How was I strong enough to get clean if I can't even figure this CEO stuff out?"

He replied, "The problem with an addict is that we'll find something that works and then stop doing it. You know how you got clean. Just do that."

It dawned on me that I never could have gotten clean without a sponsor to show me what to do. So, I decided to find someone to do that for me in my business. I needed help from someone who'd been through what I was going through. I went to my team the next day and said, "Guys, I don't know what I'm doing as CEO and I'm scared.

You're all counting on me to lead you, but I need someone to teach me right now. I need help." This went against everything I thought a strong CEO should do, but I knew my team didn't need a clueless leader with a fake CEO mask running the company. They needed a real CEO.

> **My team didn't need a clueless leader with a fake CEO mask running the company. They needed a real CEO.**

Instead of losing confidence in me and running away, they immediately jumped in and helped. They called around and found a local entrepreneur organization full of potential mentors and, a couple of weeks later, I found myself sitting in a two-day training session on how to be a CEO. One hour in, I called Kurt, my Director of Operations at the time, and said, "Kurt, we've got a problem. We don't have a CEO."

He said, "What are you talking about? *You're* the CEO!"

"No, I'm not," I replied. "That's just what my business card says. They just spent an hour explaining what a real CEO does, and I'm not doing *any* of those things."

Cautiously, Kurt said, "Uh ... okay. So, what are we going to do?"

"I'm going to go back into that training, and I'm going to learn everything I need to learn to scale this company." And I did.

If it weren't for that business mentor and that CEO training, I never would have grown into the executive that my company and my team needed me to be. Our growth would have been severely limited; it never would have grown beyond where I was equipped to take it. To take the business further, I had to take *myself* further, and that meant opening up about my weaknesses and getting the help I needed.

Now, fast forward a year later. By that point, Kurt had been promoted to COO, and he was my right-hand man in running the company. We were both lightyears ahead of where we were as leaders just a year earlier, and we were both committed to leading mask-free. However, Kurt was getting more and more stressed. He was the prototypical servant leader, always worried about everyone else and putting others ahead of himself. Without realizing it, he kept the "I'm fine" mask stuck to his face all the time, even though no one in his position would have *really* been fine under those conditions.

One day in our one-on-one meeting, I went into sponsor mode. I said, "Kurt, you're my most important leader, but I know you're not telling me everything you need to say. I keep asking what you need or want, and you keep telling me you're fine. So, let's try this instead. Let's say you come to me one year from now and quit. You tell me you're leaving the company and there's nothing I can do to change your mind. What's your best guess as to the reason why you'd be leaving?"

He smiled and sat back in his chair for a minute. Then, he replied, "It'd be because I didn't feel empowered." That surprised me so we dug into it a bit. He finally called me out for micromanaging him in one area—our patient satisfaction scores—pointing out that I wasn't giving him the trust he deserved.

I said, "Man . . . you're right. I see it now, and you are totally right. How can we fix it?"

> To take the business further, I had to take *myself* further, and that meant opening up about my weaknesses and getting the help I needed.

As a result of that conversation, we created a dashboard so everyone could see the patient satisfaction data. That not only made him happier, gave him more time back, and improved our relationship, but it also made the entire company stronger because now everyone had data that saved them time. Remember the two-way street concept I mentioned earlier? Well, this was it in practice. By sponsoring Kurt, he had actually helped *me* grow!

What I want you to see is that leading with vulnerability didn't actually cost me anything in either situation. Because I led myself in being mask-free with my team, Kurt felt confident being mask-free as well. But, since we can't spot our own self-deception, Kurt didn't even realize he was wearing a mask. He knew how to live and lead mask-free, but he still needed a sponsor to catch his blind spots. The result was reclaimed time that was wasted by people not having the information they needed, reclaimed trust that I'd lost from my micromanaging, and a reclaimed sense of true leadership because Kurt and I practiced leading ourselves and ended up innovating the way we reported data within the company. It made him better, me better, and the company better.

**When we lead ourselves in front of our people the same way a sponsor does in front of their sponsees, we end up not needing to lead our people at all.**

By being a sponsor instead of a hero, we can lead through our experience instead of strength. When our people see us say no, show weaknesses, have difficult conversations, share our unique perspective, or openly admit when we failed to do any of these things, we win a tremendous amount of trust. Everyone is free to ask the stupid question, challenge "the way we have always done it," and point out their leader's or even their own mistakes. When we lead ourselves in front of our people the same way a sponsor does in front of their sponsees, we end up not needing to lead our people at all.

## WOULD THAT BE ENOUGH?

Imagine what would happen if everyone in a company or community, starting at the top, practiced a *give it to keep it* sponsorship mindset. What if everyone worked to get mask-free and then fought to keep the masks off by teaching other people how to do it? That would be world-changing!

However, what if you try this and you don't change the world? What if you don't become incredibly successful in work, make more money, or win awards? What if nothing improves professionally at all? What if all that happens is the people you sponsor learn to lead themselves? Would that be enough?

I mentioned Archie, a guy I met early in recovery, in the previous chapter. He's the one who told me that recovery is only a program for those who *do* it. One night early in my recovery, we were talking about the twelve-step program and what I hoped to get out of it, and he said, "You know, Michael, when people get clean, they talk about what they want to get out of recovery. The want to get their job back. They want to get their spouse back. They want to get their kids back. They want to get their car back." Archie smiled. Then he asked me, "What if you don't get *anything* back? What if all you get is the ability to help just one other addict stay clean? *Just one.* Would that be enough?"

I've thought about that a lot over the years as I've tried to recover from my drug and mask addiction and help other addicts and my employees to do the same. I've asked myself, *What if I take all these risks and it doesn't improve the business? What if I invest in my people this way and they take all that reclaimed time, trust, and true leadership to another company? What if, at the end of the day, we have to shut this business down because I was more concerned about helping my team members be their true selves than I was about the bottom line? What if the only thing I get out of this is the ability to stay free of my masks and help my employees get free of theirs? Would that be enough?*

Yes, yes, yes, and yes.

Early in my career, I genuinely thought that leading this way would hurt me as a leader. It's so contrary to everything else I'd ever learned about leadership; I just assumed my commitment to living and leading mask-free while helping others do the same would limit our success. But

I didn't have a choice. My recovery forced me to lead this way. If I didn't sponsor my team in their mask addiction, I knew I would fall right back into mine. As it turned out, this new way of leading didn't limit our success; it enabled it. As I led my team from the position of a sponsor, we had so much time, trust, and true leadership that we were able to move mountains in one of the most complex and cutthroat industries in corporate America.

Not everyone is going to risk living out this program with the people in their company or community, and I can't make any promises about what will happen if you do. I can only tell you what happened when I did it and when I watched other brave leaders do it. I thought I had to choose between my team's welfare and my success. I took a risk and chose *both*. So, can you.

> **This new way of leading didn't limit our success; it enabled it.**

Many people may not be in a position to create their own mask-free culture where they work. That's okay, because the third and final piece of the Mask-Free Program, after system and sponsor, is society. In this final piece, you will learn how without society, the system and sponsor do not work, how the society will give you more support than any company or community ever could, and how, if you are a part of the Mask-Free Program, a mask-free society means you never have to live mask-free alone.

If I can make that true for just one person reading this book . . . it *would* be enough.

# CHAPTER 6

# THE MASK-FREE SOCIETY

EARLY IN MY RECOVERY FROM DRUGS AND ALCOHOL, I WAS TAUGHT, "No playmates, playgrounds, or playthings." In our world, that means to stay away from the people, places, and things that used to support our old drug and alcohol addiction—something I did by moving across the country to Nashville, Tennessee. In the first year of recovery, I spent most of my time with recovering addicts, so my environment wasn't a challenge. On the rare occasion when I was around someone who started drinking, I just removed myself from the situation. No big deal. However, once I started advancing in my career, things got a little more complicated. It became harder to stay safely tucked away in the twelve-step recovery bubble I'd gotten so comfortable in. In the working world, I had to learn how to practice my recovery around people who didn't share my new value system.

> "No playmates, playgrounds, or playthings."

At around a year and a half clean, I joined a new team at my company. Being on that team was a dream come true. It was like the

A-Team; they were an elite squad of salespeople who "ruled the school." They were always telling "war stories" from their conquests closing a big deal or their crazy nights celebrating. If the office were high school, they would have been the superstar jocks—and I'd just joined the team as the rookie freshman. One night, our boss took us out to a local bar for a team outing. I was nervous going to a bar. I was even more nervous going to a bar with a team of go-getters who I wanted to impress. They would be drinking. I wouldn't. Drinking anything—even a single drop of alcohol—was completely out of the question, but I still felt the pressure to fit in. Everyone knew I was a recovering addict, but that wasn't going to make it any easier when they started throwing the drinks back.

I called my sponsor from the parking lot before I walked in to meet everyone. I didn't want to head into battle without *someone* from my recovery community knowing where I was and what was going on. I walked in and spent the next two hours watching everyone I worked with order drink after drink. The level of fun seemed to go up in proportion to the level of alcohol they consumed. Nobody pressured me to drink, but I still felt the call. Watching them, the thoughts flew through my brain. I wanted to be that funny, and I wanted my work peers to see how awesome and fun "Party Michael" could be. Someone would comment on how smooth the vodka was, and I could feel it in the back of my throat. They started telling stories from previous nights, and I wanted to be part of those stories. I could see the buzz in their eyes as they drank, and I missed that feeling. I saw a pretty woman across the bar and longed for the liquid courage I used to have in those situations to go talk to her. I thought back to those wild, crazy days when anything could happen, when I would wake up and have no idea where I was.

This was a good group, and they were just blowing off steam after a long day at work. But it represented much more to me. It represented a life that had almost killed me, a life I'd spent almost two years recovering from. There was no way I was going back there. No one offered me a drink that night, but I still craved one—not just for the buzz, but so I could truly feel like I was a part of their society. I wanted to belong, to fit in and be known by the people I worked with.

As I sat there wrestling with the gravitational pull of my work community, I knew I had to get my head on straight. These people, as awesome as they were, weren't *my people*. Not anymore, anyway. No, *my people* were my new community of recovering addicts. They were my sponsor and the men and women in my home group. They were the people I'd see the following night at our meeting, the people I knew I would tell about my night out at the bar. The people who would completely understand how hard it was to be in that bar that night. Thinking about them, focusing on their faces and the conversation I knew I'd have with them, enabled me to power through the rest of the evening at the bar and resist the temptation to go with the flow. I knew as soon as I told them about my night out, they would immediately relate and share a story about when they went through something similar.

> I wanted to belong, to fit in and be known by the people I worked with.

I texted my sponsor and other members of my twelve-step community throughout the night. They kept me sane. Later, after I left the bar, I met several people from my home group for coffee to discuss my experience. We talked about how hard it is to change everything about our lives, to turn our backs on the things that used to feel so comfortable and to refocus all that energy into building a new life for ourselves with a new lens and new way to live. I realized that the reason I'd been so uncomfortable at the bar wasn't because I was worried about relapsing; it was because I felt so out of place there. The bar community wasn't *mine* anymore. Sitting in the coffee shop with my recovery friends, it struck me: this was my new tribe. I wanted their way of life. I wanted their value system, not the sales team's. These were the people who knew me better than anyone else, the people whose opinion mattered the most.

## NEVER ALONE

When I got clean, my twelve-step community told me I would be "never alone, never again." My community is with me ... even when they aren't with me. That sense of community is so important to all types of addicts because we can't live only in twelve-step meetings. At some point, we have to go out into the world and live in a different value system.

> My community is with me ... even when they aren't with me.

Back in those early days, I would meet with Chuck every once in a while and talk to him on the phone for less than an hour each week. Compare that to the sixty hours I spent at work with the fun-loving, bar-hopping fraternity of salespeople each week. One person, even my sponsor, as good as he was, just couldn't compete with that. But my recovery community more than made up the difference. My community gave me the power of Chuck times a hundred. It exponentially increased the power and presence of the whole recovery program in my life.

The power of the twelve steps and sponsor in a recovery program cannot be overstated. There's magic in working the life-changing program alongside a guide who's been where you are. Most people outside the recovery world think that's where the process stops. They just think of recovery as a way of learning how to live without drugs, alcohol, or whatever you might be addicted to and getting a sponsor to work with. But the twelve steps and sponsor are just two legs of the stool. Without the third leg, an entire society filled with people working the twelve steps with a sponsor, the whole program falls apart.

Like we did in the previous chapter, I want to start by discussing how this important element works in a traditional twelve-step program. As I break it down, think about how you could apply this understanding of society to your mask recovery process.

## Meeting Makers Make It

If a drug addict wants to get clean and stay clean, he has to change everything in his life. I know I did back in the day. I used to arrange my whole world around getting high. Every relationship and interaction was focused on that one goal. So, when I got clean, I knew I couldn't go back to hanging out with the same group of friends. They were all a big part of the world I was leaving behind, and I was terrified about starting this new life alone. Thankfully, that didn't turn out to be the case. Sure, I had to give up my old friends who were still using, but what I didn't count on was the fact that I'd be replacing them with an entirely new society. When I entered twelve-step recovery, I joined a new society of fellow addicts who all rallied behind a shared goal of staying clean. Without that society, I (and most recovering addicts) would fail.

> When addicts try to go at it alone, our addiction—like any predator—will usually single us out and attack.

In my twelve-step recovery, we're taught that *meeting makers make it*. This means the people who commit to regularly attend meetings and stay active in our society of fellow addicts have a much greater chance of long-term success than those who don't. There's safety in the tribe. When addicts try to go at it alone, our addiction—like any predator—will usually single us out and attack. That goes for the addict in their first month, first year, or twentieth year of recovery. Addicts who are serious about staying clean eventually accept the fact that they'll be in meetings for the rest of their lives. This often comes as a surprise to people outside recovery. Like I mentioned earlier, I had been clean for twelve years when I met my wife. She asked me early on why I still went to meetings since I'd been clean for so long. My answer was simple: "Because I want to *stay* clean."

I can practice the twelve steps night and day. I can talk to my sponsor all the time. But if I leave out the societal aspect, I'm toast. That's because my recovery—*any recovery*—is not a tactic or to-do list; it's a way of life. And, as with any way of life, we live according to the values of the society that surrounds us. If I unplug from the society that supports and encourages my twelve-step recovery lifestyle, I know all my old instincts and inclinations to use drugs will kick back in. I wish that wasn't the case, but I can't control that. What I can control is what I do about it. The fact is, I'm a drug addict, and I'll always be a drug addict. Those cravings aren't completely gone. On any given day, I might have a passing thought about using again. I don't feel the pull of drugs and alcohol anymore in my day-to-day life, but that's only because I've engineered a life that doesn't support getting high. As long as I'm actively engaged in a society that values recovery, and as long as I work the twelve steps with a sponsor within that society, my new value system will win. If I remove myself from that society, though, I'm more likely to start doing the things the larger community is doing. With liquor stores on every corner, marijuana now legal in several states, sales teams having team meetings in bars, and an opioid epidemic, the world surrounds the addict like a mob. It's a sea of people moving one way, and the recovering addict has to fight against the tide.

## Anonymous but Not Unknown

The term *anonymous* has become synonymous with twelve-step programs. Most people assume *anonymous* simply refers to our extreme level of privacy in our fellowship/society. Inside the twelve-step community, though, anonymity can have another meaning. It points to our belief in *principles over personalities*. It is the common challenge of addiction and the common solution of twelve-step recovery and its principles that bring us together. That single point of commonality is what makes us all equal. Every person within the community is going to have a different individual personality that can change. The principles behind our twelve-step program don't. What keeps us together is not our focus on our individual personalities, but on the collective principles that brought us together in the first place.

Living out this level of anonymity means we don't care who someone is, where they came from, how bad their addiction was, what they do for a living, or what mistakes they've made. To us, they are just another addict. The twelve-step society is built around the only thing we all have in common: recovery from active addiction. With that as the foundation of our relationship, it becomes incredibly safe to leave our masks at the door. Addicts are always meant to feel welcome in our meetings; their masks, however, are not. That doesn't stop people from trying to put on a false face in our community, but it usually doesn't last. It may take a while to build trust, but most people come to accept that this society *really does* want the addict to show their true face, because, if they don't, they won't stay clean.

> **Addicts are always meant to feel welcome in our meetings; their masks, however, are not.**

## Meetings, Meetings, Meetings

I've been going to meetings regularly for so long that I often forget the average person doesn't really know what happens in a twelve-step meeting. I've found that most people assume a meeting is just a forum for addicts to air their dirty laundry or wallow in their addiction. Meetings *can* include that, but it's not the ultimate goal. There's no point in just focusing on the problem of addiction; everyone in the room knows that problem all too well. What many do not have is the *solution*. So, we try to focus on how we are applying the twelve-step program not just to our addiction, but to life on life's terms.

In my experience, here's how meetings usually go. They last about an hour, and there are no hard limits on the number of attendees. I've been in meetings with two people and even attended meetings with thousands. There are many formats, but one of the most common is a meeting where anyone who wants to share is welcome to, meaning they talk for around five minutes. Shares vary, but I've found they usually fall into one of three types. Participants may:

1. Share a problem.
2. Share their experience, applying the program to a problem.
3. Share an experience living the program.

The common denominator here is the twelve-step program. A meeting is an opportunity to talk about the ups and downs of using our shared program in different situations.

When someone shares a challenge, others will often follow up by sharing an experience they had facing a similar struggle and how they used the program to overcome it. This is *not* telling someone else what they should do; it's simply one addict sharing a personal experience using the program. For example, someone will share that they're struggling because they are going through a divorce and having trouble surrendering. Then, someone else may follow and say, "I can relate to the last share. When I was fighting for custody of my child, I really struggled to let go of what the court system was doing. I called my sponsor, and she reminded me that I couldn't control anyone other than myself. She also suggested I identify the step that I needed to apply to the situation and come to this meeting to share." The key is that no one is giving direct advice or speaking directly to another member. They're just saying, "I can relate to that struggle. Here's my experience applying the twelve steps to a similar issue."

We also share successes, such as when someone gets their children back or when I was able to go to my team outing at a bar with a bunch of salespeople and not relapse. These shares also show others what's possible, which is a huge encouragement. Every member of the group may have completely different external circumstances and problems, but, during the course of a meeting, we are reminded that we have a common internal problem and a common internal solution. We are reminded, no matter who shares, that we can apply the twelve steps to anything in our lives.

## BENEFITS OF THE RECOVERY SOCIETY

Helen Keller once said, "Alone we can do so little; together we can do so much." Nowhere is that truer, in my experience, than in recovery. In fact, I might even take it further: Alone we can't do *anything*, but together we can do *everything*. I owe my life to my twelve-step society. Over the past seventeen years in this society, I not only stayed clean, but I found the answer to every single challenge I've faced. It is truly an incredible resource that has improved my life in every way. I could talk for days about the benefits I've experienced by being connected to this kind of society, but for now I'll mention the three with the greatest impact:

1. Society provides a common language and goal.
2. Society realigns our perceptions of ourselves and the world.
3. Society gives us infinite experience to draw on.

Let's take a quick look at each benefit.

### Common Language and Goals

First, the society provides a common language and goal. I can walk into a twelve-step meeting in any city in the country and know exactly what's going on with no prep and without ever meeting any of the attendees beforehand. Our society creates an enormous amount of efficiency, because the only introduction any group needs to hear from me is, "Hi.

I'm Michael, I'm a drug addict, and I'm struggling with Step One." That's it. That's all they need to know about me. From then on, I know they're going to understand anything I share in the meeting because we're all coming at this from the same place with the same language, the same goal, and the same program.

A shared goal also creates trust. This means I can share absolutely anything in a meeting with no fear of the group's shock or criticism. Our masks try to isolate us but sharing with that level of openness and honesty inherently rips the masks right off our faces. That enables us to share our true selves—the struggles *and* the victories. When I sold InQuicker, for example, I was hesitant to share how I was struggling to enjoy it and how terrified I was of managing my new resources. Many of my fellow addicts were working minimum-wage jobs. The last thing I

**A shared goal also creates trust.**

wanted to do was to go into a meeting and complain about *having* money. But that's the beauty of a society like the one I was in. They didn't care how much I had or how little I had. They were fellow addicts and, when I eventually shared my concerns, they shared similar experiences of receiving blessings but feeling guilty and not knowing what to do with them.

This is a great example of how addiction and masks separate us from the people we need the most. I was scared to share something. But, thanks to the common language and common goal, that fear melted away. I remember talking to my friend Toby about my concern after the meeting, and he said, "What's happening on the outside doesn't matter nearly as much as what happens on the inside. You may be in a different situation than I am, but we are both equally susceptible to fear and pain. This is an inside job and, in order to do that job, we share what's going on no matter what." What we have in common gives us a level of safety to be vulnerable, and that makes our meetings the total opposite of a typical business meeting.

## The Power of Perception

Second, society realigns our perception of ourselves and the world. When I'm out in the world every day, in the world's value system, I can find my thinking and perception change. I find myself living in more fear, comparing myself to others, scared things won't go my way, attached to outcomes, chasing material things, and trying to control things I can't.

By the time I sit down in a twelve-step meeting, I may have even convinced myself that I am a unique snowflake and that no one in the meeting will be able to relate. Then, people start to share, and I get flooded with an entirely different lens through which to see life. They share the things I once knew but forgot. They share situations that may be different externally, but I can completely relate to how they think and feel internally. I stop focusing so much on material things. I switch from fear to faith. I stop seeing the *differences* between myself and others, and I start seeing the *similarities*. I start letting go of the outcomes. My fellow addicts reflect back to me our common lens and reinforce our shared values. Suddenly, my perception has completely changed.

> Society realigns our perceptions of ourselves and the world.

This reflection doesn't just *help* me, it *illuminates* me. I mentioned earlier that it's nearly impossible to spot our own self-deception. Well, when others share and act as a mirror, I am not only reminded of our value system, but I am able to see parts of myself that weren't visible before. I've had so many moments in my recovery when I totally wanted to point my finger at someone and call them out for not doing something the way I thought they should. Then, they would share in the meeting and I would hear myself in their story. In those moments, I realized I hadn't been pointing my finger at them at all. I was pointing it at myself. In the same way, I can't tell you how many times someone would share something they were doing to work on themselves and I would think, *Crap. Now I need to work on that too.* Every time I walk out of a meeting, for better or worse, I am always able to see myself more clearly.

Listening to other people share also reminds us that we have a disease. After staying clean for a while, it can be easy to forget how things really were when we were using, and we can take the fundamentals of our recovery for granted. This can cause people who have been clean for ten years to stop going to meetings. More often than not, they end up using again because they get away from the thing that got them clean in the first place. By keeping the society front and center, though, we're constantly reminded that addiction is a lifelong disease and something we can never take for granted. Plus, hearing newcomers share about their intense fight to get clean is a powerful reminder that I *should* be dead, and that this life-changing program saved me. Few things reset my perception as effectively as that.

## Infinite Experience

Third, the society provides all the experiences an addict will ever need to make it through his recovery. We saw in the previous chapter that sponsors don't tell their sponsees what to do; they only share experiences. But the sponsor only has *one set of experiences* to draw from. The society, on the other hand, represents an endless number of experiences ready to be shared. Whatever an addict is going through, he's sure to find someone in the society who has already been through it and is willing to share their experiences.

> Every time I walk out of a meeting, for better or worse, I am always able to see myself more clearly.

I call this *infinite experience.* Everyone is on the same path, with addicts ahead of them, addicts behind them, and addicts to the side of them. Every single addict in the program is surrounded by recovering addicts with so many different experiences. My closest friends have anywhere from ten to thirty-five years clean, and each one of them has a sponsor who has a sponsor who has a sponsor. And each one has a sponsee who has a sponsee. When I walk into my home group meeting, I am not only spending time with the fifty-plus people who are my friends; collectively, we are connected to an incredible network that represents centuries upon centuries of experience working the program. There is nothing I will face in life where I can't tap into that infinite experience and get guidance on how to face whatever I am going through. It's just one meeting, coffee, or phone call away. And, when I spend ten or more hours per day surrounded by people who don't have a clue what addiction is really like, you can't imagine how powerful just one hour in that twelve-step society is.

> Society provides all the experiences an addict will ever need to make it through his recovery.

Now that I've explained the drug addiction side of a recovery community, let's see what these principles could mean for your mask recovery.

## SECRET AGENTS IN A MASKED SOCIETY

Our society, in its most basic form, is the people we surround ourselves with. For those of us who are employed, this is often our work society because those are the people we potentially spend most of our time with. These people make up our modern-day tribe. It's not exactly how the cavemen did it, but it's close. We travel in packs, work in teams, and put all our energy into acquiring resources for our families. In a real way, we depend on our work tribe for our survival—even in the twenty-first century.

The problem is, the work society we spend so much time with most likely has masked values. It can feel impossible to stay mask-free if the pack we're running with is wearing masks, thinking it will make them more successful. That was certainly my experience when I got my first real job at a major company. I started spending more than forty hours a week with people who were doing the complete opposite of practicing rigorous authenticity, surrendering the outcome, and doing uncomfortable work. I found myself desperately hoping I could find other recovering drug addicts in my office. I felt like a secret agent hiding in the professional world, and I longed for the friendly face of a fellow secret agent. I yearned to find someone who had the same value system, someone I could be real with.

You can only stay behind enemy lines for so long. We've all seen movies about an undercover cop who goes so deep into the drug lifestyle and society that he ends up getting lost in it. You know those movies, right? After a while, you start identifying as part of that society, and you lose yourself to it. That was my fear. I was afraid of losing myself to the masked culture I saw around me at work. Like we say in recovery, "If you hang out in a barbershop long enough, you're going to get your hair cut." Everything I was seeing and everything I'd ever been taught outside of recovery said that I needed to wear a mask at work in order to be successful. Refusing to put that mask on, I feared, would jeopardize my ability to earn an income and provide for myself. That's why my twelve-step society was so important. It not only helped me stay clean, but it gave me the confidence to be mask-free at work because I still had my own society to go back to.

Maybe comparing your office to going behind enemy lines is taking it too far. I doubt you work for an international illegal drug cartel, but the workplace *is* the grown-up equivalent of high school. There are the stuffy, unapproachable "grown-ups" who tell you what to do, the bullies who make you feel an inch tall, the cliques who make you feel left out and unworthy, the popular people who seem to have it all going for them, and the loners who can't seem to catch a break. And, of course, there's peer pressure. *So much pressure* to put on the masks, to be *this* person and to fit *that* mold. I hated it when I was fourteen. I hate it even more today.

As I have coached thousands of people across different industries, work environments, and communities, I've found that this pressure exists everywhere. Whether you are a CEO, executive, manager, front-line employee, entrepreneur, self-employed, remote worker, stay-at-home parent, and so on, you almost certainly feel the pressure to wear a mask when you interact with other humans. As hard as you may want to pull the masks off, there's a good chance everyone around you is subtly (or not so subtly) encouraging you to keep it on. Remember how I said addicts are told to stay away from their old playground, playmates, and playthings? Well, inside your company or community is the masked version of each, and the power of this society is working against you by:

> **You can only stay behind enemy lines for so long.**

- ✦ Providing a masked common language and goal.
- ✦ Realigning our masked perceptions of ourselves and the world.
- ✦ Giving us infinite mask experience to draw on.

Everywhere online or offline, we can see the explicit and implicit messages that remind us to manage how we are perceived. We're taught how we look is what matters most. Our common language and common goal are to wear the mask. We then take all those messages and realign our perceptions of ourselves through that lens. We believe who we are is not enough. That we need to change ourselves. That we can't say no. That we should avoid difficult conversations. That we should hide our weaknesses. That we should hold back our unique perspectives. And when we reach out to the world for help, there are endless masked members of this society willing to offer their suggestions on what to do or how to wear the mask just right.

**Everywhere online or offline, we can see the explicit and implicit messages that remind us to manage how we are perceived.**

So, societies can work *for* you or work *against* you. If you can align yourself with a mask-free society the same way I aligned myself with my twelve-step community, you can successfully keep your mask off at work the same way I did in that bar. And, if you can successfully keep your mask off at work, you will build a strong mask-free muscle that you will be able to use *anywhere*. Alone, you can't live mask-free, but together *we* can.

## IS A MASK-FREE SOCIETY EVEN POSSIBLE AT WORK?

Early in my career, I never imagined a mask-free society was even possible in the workplace. I spent the first few years of my professional life feeling so lonely at work. I searched for my coworkers', bosses', and customers' ability to practice rigorous authenticity, but instead I would just get their masks. I had plenty of relationships with good people, but the depth of connection just wasn't there. I didn't actually use the mask language then, but I knew something was missing, something I didn't have a name for but knew I needed.

In contrast, my connection to my fellow recovering addicts always happened quickly and ran so deep. I always felt known. I never felt alone. We shared the same language, the same goal, and the same experience. We even had the 3Ts (time, trust, true leadership). When I compare the two dynamics, I became obsessed with wanting to create a recovery society at work.

My first attempt at a mask-free professional environment was when I started going to professional meetups, workshops, and mastermind groups. Some of these groups were *good*, but none was *great*. After the incredible life-change I'd experienced through my recovery, all these professional groups fell flat. Most of the people I met were nice and well intentioned, and many even desired the level of connection I was looking for, but everyone was using a different language and pursuing different goals. It was disappointing. There was no equivalent of "Hi, I'm Michael. I'm a drug addict and I'm struggling with Step One." We just didn't have the rapid connection and understanding that I had in twelve-step recovery.

### The Epiphany

In retrospect, I know exactly what was missing: the professional groups I participated in had no common system, no sponsor guidance, and no society of people with a common purpose.

In short, there was no *program*. I was looking for the recovery model among people who had never experienced it. And, as it turned out, I was sitting with a group of mask addicts who hadn't yet faced their mask addiction or didn't have the tools to achieve mask-free recovery. It dawned on me that the thing I was looking for in the professional world simply didn't exist…yet. I realized that if I couldn't find what I needed, I'd have to create it myself.

> I was sitting with a group of mask addicts who hadn't yet faced their mask addiction or didn't have the tools to achieve mask-free recovery.

When I finally left my Fortune 50 job to launch InQuicker, I was starting with a clean slate. I was the leader, and I could build the company however I wanted to. I didn't intentionally build a mask-free society at InQuicker. I didn't sit down on the first day and say, "Now, how can I make sure everyone I hire removes their masks and never feels pressure to put one back on?" I didn't even intentionally lead anyone by the three principles I outlined in chapter 4. I didn't know how to implement *any* of that on purpose with people who weren't drug addicts, and I certainly didn't know how to be a CEO. I did, however, know how to be a recovering drug addict. I knew how to work a recovery program. I knew how to practice rigorous authenticity, surrender the outcome, and do uncomfortable work. And now, away from the mask-entrenched culture of a big company, I had the chance to do all these things boldly and out in the open at work. I was able to live and lead however I wanted to in my new business. I was free to build the mask-free culture I yearned for.

With no fears about what *the boss* would say (since I *was* the boss), that's what I did. I didn't hide my weaknesses. I said no when I needed to. I didn't avoid difficult conversations when they were necessary. And, most importantly, I didn't hide my unique perspective. In fact, *I leaned into it*! And, when I did this, I noticed it made it easier for my leaders to do it too. They didn't hide *their* weaknesses. They said no when *they* needed to say no. They didn't avoid difficult conversations. They didn't hide *their* unique perspectives, and so on. Our example cascaded down to the next levels of the organization and everyone in every part of the company was bought into this radical, authentic way to live, lead, and work. We ended up with a team of fifty people working in a mask-free society, a mask-free company culture. As I built and led InQuicker to that eventual acquisition, I was just doing what my twelve-step program had taught me and, for the first time in my addiction or recovery, I didn't feel alone at work. I was surrounded by a group of beautiful human beings, all living and leading mask-free.

## Creating or Finding Your Own Mask-Free Society

As leaders, we sometimes have a tendency to wait for our people to come to us with their challenges. Then, we perk up and say, "How can I help? I'm here to coach you." By waiting for someone to come to us with their struggles and not going to them with our struggles first, we lose the opportunity to communicate that this is a safe place for them to show their true selves. If they aren't sure their leader believes in practicing rigorous authenticity as a means for success, they are right to fear that their leader may see it as a weakness and a liability. If they can't see us as intentional, contributing members of the society we're promoting, they won't trust us enough to live it out for themselves.

For example, there was a period during my time at the Fortune 50 company when the recession was killing us. We faced a downturn and had to lay some people off. It was a horrible year. Instead of waiting for individuals to bring their concerns to me, I brought mine to them. I was up front with them about how hard that time was for me. I also tried to eliminate any fear by telling them whatever details I was able to share. I'd say, "Listen, I'm struggling with this environment as well. I'm afraid of losing my job just like you probably are. So, I have had to look at this through the lens of what I can control and what I can't control, and here is what I am personally doing to get through this." Of course, there are times when we as leaders can't share all the details, but we can't use that as an excuse to hide behind our mask.

> By waiting for someone to come to us with their struggles and not going to them with our struggles first, we lose the opportunity to communicate that this is a safe place for them to show their true selves.

Our hardest moments are the greatest opportunities to establish a level of trust that transcends work. A leader may not be able to share every detail, but she can absolutely share how she feels and how she is leading herself. The hard times present an opportunity to demonstrate our commitment to a mask-free society in a way that isn't possible in the good times.

As CEO of InQuicker, I was even more proactive in being vulnerable with my team. Every week, I shared my biggest challenge, what I couldn't and could control, and what my uncomfortable work was. In time, my employees got the message that it was safe to do the same. Eventually, I didn't need to go first to make them feel safe. People started to share their challenges and uncomfortable work naturally. For example, someone would share about something a customer requested that they simply didn't understand and how tempted they were to strap on a mask in front of the customer, their team, and leadership. But, instead of wearing the mask and limiting their ability to meet the request, they brought it to our team, and we figured it out together. Other times, someone would share something much more personal, like a difficult breakup with a significant other, and discuss the uncomfortable work they were dreading. Whatever it was, everyone at every level in the company felt welcome and empowered to share with our society. It really felt like a twelve-step meeting, because we were all sharing our experiences working the Mask-Free Program.

**The hard times present an opportunity to demonstrate our commitment to a mask-free society in a way that isn't possible in the good times.**

I coach CEOs who see what we had at InQuicker and wonder why people aren't living mask-free in their company. It's because, in order to create a mask-free culture, you need mechanisms that allow it to scale. You need the Mask-Free Program the same way you need mechanisms to scale your core product or service. That kind of companywide change usually starts at the top and cascades just like everything else.

Now, I realize most people are not as lucky as I was. I was able to build a mask-free society from the ground up inside my company. Most of us, though, are either working inside someone else's organization, working on our own, or simply living in a larger community. So, how do you find your own mask-free society?

We have seen mini-mask-free societies built within larger masked societies just like I did in my corporate job with my team. We have also seen individuals in a community come together to form their own mask-free society within the larger community. Either way, it comes down to Principle 2: Surrender the Outcome. Most of us cannot control the society we live or work in just like recovering drug addicts can't stop

> In order to create a mask-free culture, you need mechanisms that allow it to scale.

our larger society from using alcohol and drugs. What we *can* control is whether we choose to be part of a smaller society that supports our new mask-free way of life.

Don't stress if you don't know how to make this happen. For now, all that matters is whether you have the desire to join a mask-free society. Whether it's a society made up of your team, coworkers, friends, or other like-minded people in your company or community, I will cover more detailed strategies for putting all this in motion in the following chapter.

## THE SHOW MUST (NOT) GO ON

The traditional leadership paradigms we have been taught aren't working anymore. It's time to take the mask off and revolutionize the rules of leadership. In a world where many of us feel disconnected, we can create an environment at work that teaches and empowers us to live mask-free when we're working *and* when we're not. Think about what an inverse that would be. We used to put the mask on when we went to work and take it off when we got home. But now that technology has taken over our lives, we just live with the mask on all the time. We're never free to be our true selves because someone is always watching. We're drowning in apps and websites that promise to give us greater connection to our friends, family, and the entire global community, but all these new connections have left us feeling more alone and isolated than ever. Sometimes it feels like we're onstage performing 24/7 when all we really want to do is collapse on a sofa with a few close friends and let our guard down for a while. But we can't. The show must go on.

That's how I felt at the height of my drug use. I did everything I could to keep up the act just one more day...until I simply couldn't do it anymore. Imagine my surprise when recovery turned out to be the way to get the very thing I'd been looking for all along: a genuine society of people who saw and accepted the real me. They *got* me because each of them was just like I was. We were all following the twelve-step program—addicts working the steps with a sponsor within a society of other people doing the same thing.

**Now that technology has taken over our lives, we just live with the mask on all the time.**

You may never know what it's like to battle a drug or alcohol addiction. I really hope you never find out. But that doesn't mean you can't experience the kind of close-knit community I discovered in recovery. That doesn't mean you can never experience the safety and security of a society that actively supports and encourages your commitment to mask-free living. Here's a radical thought: What if *work* was the place you could take your mask off? What if that's where you could practice taking it off and teach others to do the same? At InQuicker, I often told my team that we were all corporate refugees, and we were all responsible for building something different than the stuffy, isolated business environments we'd all come from. Our goal was to change the world by building a different culture that allowed us to change ourselves. And we did that together.

Now it's your turn. Do you feel the level of connection and trust that I feel among my fellow addicts in my home group? Or, do you feel more like I did at the bar that night with my coworkers? I'm here to tell you that you never have to hide behind the mask again. It is possible to learn this Mask-Free Program and live in a mask-free society, a society that unlocks the power of the true you. A society that helps you rip off the mask and break it in half.

I have taught you the Mask-Free Program. You have learned the power of the mask-free system, sponsor, and society while seeing what is possible when you use them together as one program. But, at this point, you probably aren't quite sure what to do with this vision or how exactly to implement this new way

Here's a radical thought: What if *work* was the place you could take your mask off?

of leading. Don't worry. For now, I am your mask-free sponsor, and it will be my pleasure to show you how to put this program to work for you, no matter who you are or where you work (or don't work). We'll lay out a plan for implementing this program in the following chapter. Just promise me you will keep coming back, and I will promise you a new, mask-free way of life.

# CHAPTER 7

# IT ONLY WORKS IF YOU WORK IT

Over the past few chapters, I have outlined the Mask-Free Program and its three distinct parts: the system, sponsor, and society. But it doesn't stop with just learning each part on its own. All three work together to form a program that will empower you to live and lead mask-free. The Mask-Free Program only requires about one minute a day in order to change the way you live. You can totally do this. *Anyone* can do this, and, in this chapter, I am going to show you how.

But right now, you might be somewhere between "I'm ready to go!" and "Man, this seems really hard." You might even be thinking, *Wait, this seems so simple that I don't even need an implementation plan.* All these responses are normal. Early in my recovery from drugs, I learned that just because something is *simple* doesn't mean that it is *easy.* Yes, this is a simple program; I promised you that right from the start. But that doesn't mean it's easy. Oftentimes, the most difficult thing in the world is to do something simple over and over.

The Mask-Free Program works the same way for *everyone,* whether or not your company or community are part of the Mask-Free Movement.

This book will give you a comprehensive program you can put to work immediately, but there are additional resources I'll point you to online at www.maskfreeprogram.com. That's also where you'll connect with me and, more importantly, connect with the mask-free society.

Fair warning before we get into the nuts and bolts of implementing this program: when you put this stuff into practice, you will be on the cutting edge of leadership. Some of the people around you won't notice much at first. The number one problem I run into when I am doing my workshops and coaching is that people already think they are "authentic" because of that one time in that one meeting a year ago when they "kept it real." That's a lot like when I was in active addiction and, to prove I didn't have a problem, I would always point back to that one night in 2001 when I went to bed with no substances in my body (unlike the other 364 nights that year). One of the hardest parts of addiction is self-deception. Many people will say they don't have a problem with masks, but, when you start working the Mask-Free Program—using the system, sponsor, and society as you practice rigorous authenticity, surrender the outcome, and do uncomfortable work as if your life depended on it—there is going to be a huge difference between you and the people around you over time. So, when you start talking about working the Mask-Free Program, it may sound weird to them. That's good. It gives you a competitive advantage.

> **Oftentimes, the most difficult thing in the world is to do something simple over and over.**

The key to living and leading mask-free begins and ends with working the three-part Mask-Free Program I've laid out through this book:

1. Work the System
2. Get a Sponsor
3. Join a Society

Now I want to make the implementation as simple and clear as the program itself, so I'm going to put on my sponsor hat and guide you through these three parts. At the end of each part, I'll give you a checklist of specific actions.

# PART I: WORK THE SYSTEM

Let's start by unpacking how to implement the system we discussed in chapter 4. There are four steps to this part of the Mask-Free Program:

1. Complete the 3 Principle Worksheets
2. Create an Action Card
3. Perform a One-Minute Daily Inventory
4. Start your recurring 28-Day Action Plan

## Step 1: Complete the Three Principle Worksheets

Remember how I told you back in chapter 4 that you would get an opportunity to refine your answers? Here it is! I am going to guide you through the system one more time using the three principle worksheets included in this chapter. Your answers may be the same as they were originally, but don't be surprised if something changes. Write your answers in the book for now. You can find additional worksheets at www.maskfreeprogram.com.

## Worksheet 1: Practice Rigorous Authenticity

Start with the Principle 1: Practice Rigorous Authenticity worksheet. This sheet targets the mask you need to address, the fear that causes you to wear it, and the cost of wearing it. Feel free to refer back to the instructions in chapter 4 on pages 96–97 as you work through the following worksheet.

## Worksheet 1: Practice Rigorous Authenticity

My mask is:

My fear is:

My professional costs:

My personal costs:

My long-term costs:

**Worksheet 2: Surrender the Outcome**

Next is the Principle 2: Surrender the Outcome worksheet. The goal for this worksheet is to identify the outcome(s) you want or that you want to avoid, as well as what you *can't* and *can* control. You can refer to the instructions on pages 97–99 as you work through the following worksheet.

**Worksheet 2: Surrender the Outcome**

The outcome(s):

I *can't* control:      I *can* control:

**Worksheet 3: Do Uncomfortable Work**
Focusing on your CAN list prepares you for the Principle 3: Do Uncomfortable Work worksheet. Here, you will identify the specific actions you need to take. Refer to the instructions on pages 99–102 as you answer the questions in the following worksheet.

**Worksheet 3: Do Uncomfortable Work**

My uncomfortable work:

Throughout this chapter I will keep reinforcing this point: the key to the Mask-Free Program is *repetition*, and completing this work a second time here gives you your second rep. As you get more comfortable targeting your masks in this way, it will get easier for you to run through these worksheets in just a few minutes.

**My sister has always been one of my biggest fans.** I love you, Brooke.

**Me, around eight years old.** Who would have thought this
kid would be teaching leaders to live like drug addicts?

**My buddy Aaron and I during our freshman year of college.** This dude (and his couch) saved me from sleeping on the streets.

**Brooke and I, 1999.** I always tried to corrupt Brooke with alcohol, drugs, bad music, and *Family Guy*. None of it took. She's an incredible woman.

**My dad and I.** This picture was taken when I was "digitizing paperwork" for my parents. A year later, my dad took me to dinner and offered to send me to rehab.

**Drunk and high in 2002.** My only focus was to stay drunk and high at any cost. I pass around this picture in my home group every year to celebrate being clean.

**Also drunk and high in 2002.** I was sleeping on Aaron's couch at the time. He bought me food and cigarettes each day, and I stole from him when he wasn't looking.

**Sleeping on Aaron's floor in my daily uniform.** Aaron had a friend come to stay for a weekend, so the least I could do was give up the couch.

**Boyce.** After landing in Nashville, TN, for an extended rehab, Boyce picked me up at the airport. He's the first old-timer whom I learned from.

**I love my parents.** And, even though I put them through hell, they have always believed in me.

**My manager, Patrick, and I, corporate job, 2004.**
I received a huge award that night, and Patrick, who knew
my story, called my parents while presenting it to me.

**Chuck and I at a New Year's party in 2004.** While I was breakdancing for the
crowd, Chuck and our friend Emily were setting off a confetti bomb in my car.

**Chuck's wife, Holly, and I, 2006.** Holly is a mother-figure, best friend, and spiritual advisor to me. In 2010, she started working at InQuicker as our director of finance.

**Chuck and I on my five-year clean-time anniversary.** Chuck loves to make a big deal out of recovery milestones, and I was the beneficiary of that.

**The first team offsite meeting at InQuicker.** It included a meal at Waffle House, plans to reinvent access to healthcare, and then a movie.

**Kurt and I at InQuicker, around 2013.** Kurt was my first manager in corporate America and the first employee I hired at InQuicker. He and his wife, Jenny, are like family to me.

**InQuicker billboards.** We had billboards all over the nation and were so grateful that our hospital partners advertised our product in such a significant way.

Mike —

Every CEO will make that mistake. Very few, however, will take action as you did to fix it. I love you; and I'm always thankful for the example you set. Sincerely,

Adam

InQuicker.com

**One of the best gifts I ever received as CEO of InQuicker.**
Adam West, one of our leaders, witnessed me fail as a leader,
yet he still wrote me this note that I look at often.

**Inc. 500 awards ceremony.** The ceremony was such a weird experience because while representing our company in such a public way, I was also fighting to remain a part of it.

**My entrepreneur group in Chicago.** These guys went out of their way to help me through my year of divorces. EO Forum 13/14, I love you guys for life!

**Chuck, Holly, and I in Mexico, Christmas 2014.** I had just found out that I would be taking my company back over and was celebrating with two of my favorite people.

**My friend Erica and I.** She is the only friend with whom I experienced high school, college, and InQuicker together. I am so grateful for her love and support.

**Elizabeth and I, early 2015.** Who would have thought fresh off of divorces with my ex-wife and business partner I would fall in love with my future wife and business partner?

**The entire InQuicker team, 2015.** Taken on the night we celebrated being acquired. Words cannot express how grateful I am for each of these beautiful people.

**Toby and I in Hawaii, 2016.** When I first met Toby, I told him he was going to be my best friend. We help each other in so many areas, and he is always my best advisor.

**Stacie and I.** Stacie was my head of marketing at InQuicker, and now we have joined forces again to launch another startup, the Mask-Free Movement!

**Elizabeth and I on our wedding day, 2018.** I can't believe I get to partner with my wife at work, as parents, and in life. I love you, EBW!

**TEDx Talk, "Great Leaders Do What Drug Addicts Do," March 2018.**
The talk that started it all. I am so honored to be able to carry this message.

**My daughter, Amorette.** Being a parent is hard, but the more I see this beautiful human take shape, the more I appreciate just how worth it all of this is.

**MBW, EBW, and ABW.** The only Brody-Waites on earth (thanks to my sister giving up her maiden name), we are embracing our unique perspective. I love you, BWs!

## Step 2: Create Your Action Card

The work you have completed prepares you to fill out the most important tool in this system: the Action Card. This tool is where we go from *inspiration* to *implementation*!

The goal of the Action Card is to distill your insights from the worksheets into small, actionable statements. You want these statements to be concise enough to fit on the card and clear enough to know exactly what you're working towards. We're aiming for clarity, not complexity. That's why the participants in my workshops don't leave with a two-inch binder; they leave with a simple 4x6-inch Action Card. This is what makes this system so portable. You can literally carry the entire system in your pocket.

To help guide your implementation, I am going to show you a blank action card (on the next page), explain how to fill it out out and give you four examples to reference. At any point, if you need help, you can refer to the sample cards at the end of this section.

The Action Card is designed to clearly tell you at a glance:

1. What mask you're wearing (Principle 1: Practice Rigorous Authenticity)
2. What you *can't* and *can* control (Principle 2: Surrender the Outcome)
3. What action(s) you need to take (Principle 3: Do Uncomfortable Work)
4. Your *why*

Now, let's talk through how you fill it out.

### Principle 1: Practice Rigorous Authenticity

Refer to your Principle 1 worksheet from earlier in this chapter and simply write the same mask you wrote there on your Action Card. Don't worry about the other content on your worksheet for now. We'll get to that later.

# MASK-FREE ACTION CARD

## 1. PRACTICE RIGOROUS AUTHENTICITY
My mask is


## 2. SURRENDER THE OUTCOME

I *can't* control | I *can* control


## 3. DO THE UNCOMFORTABLE WORK
My Daily Reflection


My Mask-Free Action(s)


## WHY THIS MATTERS TO ME

**Principle 2: Surrender the Outcome**

Refer to your Principle 2 worksheet and write simple phrases for what you CAN'T control on the left and what you CAN control on the right.

**Principle 3: Do Uncomfortable Work**

For "My Daily Reflection," look at your mask and write the mask-free version in the form of a question. For example, if your mask is "Saying yes when I could say no," your daily reflection would be "Did I say no today?" Again, feel free to refer to the examples at the end of this section for help.

For the "Mask-Free Action(s)" section, look at all of your uncomfortable work and write what you will do over the next twenty-eight days to live mask-free. Try to make these actions as specific as possible. Also, I wouldn't recommend writing more than two or three.

Then, at the bottom of the Action Card, you'll write down your *why*. Why does this work matter to you? Think back to the professional and personal costs we discussed in Principle 1. Think about the long-term costs. Think about the costs of time, trust, and true leadership. Then wrap it all up in a statement that incorporates your deathbed perspective. Your *why* statement has to be motivating. For example, on one of my Action Cards, the mask I identified is "Saying yes when I could say no." It costs me plenty personally and professionally, but what motivates me the most is when I think long term. So, taking my deathbed perspective into account, my *why* is, "On my deathbed, being there for my wife and daughter will matter most." That may sound grim, but it's a huge motivator for me.

You are the only person who will know what the mask costs you and what will motivate you to take it off. Look back over your worksheets and think through the reason you bought this book in the first place. All that matters is that your *why* motivates you. Besides, you can't do this wrong because you are going to do it over and over again. All that practice and iteration will teach you what works best for you over time.

That's it! Now that you know how to fill out an Action Card, here are some examples that might help you refine yours over time.

# MASK-FREE ACTION CARD

## 1. PRACTICE RIGOROUS AUTHENTICITY

My mask is

Saying yes when I could say no

## 2. SURRENDER THE OUTCOME

| I *can't* control | I *can* control |
|---|---|
| That my time is a limited resource | If I spend my time on my most important priorities |
| How people respond when I decline or delegate a request | How I decline or delegate a request |

## 3. DO THE UNCOMFORTABLE WORK

My Daily Reflection

Did I say no today?

My Mask-Free Action(s)

1. Review my calendar, projects, and tasks
2. List any requests misaligned with my priorities
3. Decline or delegate at least 3 of them

## WHY THIS MATTERS TO ME

I want my kids to remember me taking them to school

# MASK-FREE ACTION CARD

## 1. PRACTICE RIGOROUS AUTHENTICITY
My mask is
Hiding a weakness

## 2. SURRENDER THE OUTCOME

| I *can't* control | I *can* control |
|---|---|
| That I am weak in a specific area | If I ask for what I need to improve my weakness |
| What people will think of me when I share my weakness | If I take the steps to improve |

## 3. DO THE UNCOMFORTABLE WORK
My Daily Reflection
Did I share a weakness today?

My Mask-Free Action(s)
1. Identify any weaknesses I would like to improve
2. Share my weakness with someone who can help
3. Take the steps to improve

## WHY THIS MATTERS TO ME
I want to be the best version of myself

# MASK-FREE ACTION CARD

## 1. PRACTICE RIGOROUS AUTHENTICITY

My mask is
Avoiding difficult conversations

## 2. SURRENDER THE OUTCOME

| I *can't* control | I *can* control |
|---|---|
| How others respond to difficult conversations | If I address challenges and take the steps to make issues known |
| The result of the difficult conversation | How I communicate in a difficult conversation |

## 3. DO THE UNCOMFORTABLE WORK

My Daily Reflection
Did I have a difficult conversation today?

My Mask-Free Action(s)
1. Review my relationships
2. List any difficult conversations I am avoiding
3. Choose 2 difficult conversations and have them

## WHY THIS MATTERS TO ME

I want to stop carrying around resentment

# MASK-FREE ACTION CARD

## 1. PRACTICE RIGOROUS AUTHENTICITY

My mask is
Holding back my unique perspective

## 2. SURRENDER THE OUTCOME

| I *can't* control | I *can* control |
|---|---|
| What others think of my perspective | If I create an opportunity to make an impact |
| If my perspective makes an impact | How I communicate my perspective |

## 3. DO THE UNCOMFORTABLE WORK

My Daily Reflection
Did I share my unique perspective today?

My Mask-Free Action(s)
1. Review my interactions in work and life
2. List any unique perspectives I have held back
3. Choose 1 unique perspective and share it

## WHY THIS MATTERS TO ME
I don't want to regret not speaking up

Something magical happens when we write our goals on paper. It turns an ephemeral ideal into something physical. It pulls a dream out of the clouds and puts it in black and white right in front of us. Simply putting it on paper doesn't make it valuable, though. Paper is only valuable because of the value we *ascribe* to it. When I get a piece of junk mail, I tear it up and throw it in the recycling because it means nothing to me. It's just wasted paper. On the other hand, how great does it feel to open the mail and find a $50, $100, or $1,000 check waiting inside? Maybe it's a birthday gift, a refund from an accidental overpayment, or a tax refund. Would you tear up that check? I sure wouldn't. Why? I mean, a check is just a piece of paper that unexpectedly appears in my mailbox. It's no different than junk mail—except for the value we have given it.

> **Your Action Card can be scrap paper, or it can be the thing that fundamentally transforms your life.**

In the same way, your Action Card can be scrap paper, or it can be the thing that fundamentally transforms your life. When I teach this in workshops, we laminate every participant's card as soon as he or she writes it in order to protect it and symbolize its importance.

One last reminder about the Action Cards: There are more masks than the four we talk about in this book. As you grow in your Mask-Free Program, you can take our assessment to identify additional masks to work on at www.maskfreeprogram.com. You will also be able to find more Action Card templates and Action Card examples there as well.

### Step 3: Perform a One-Minute Daily Inventory

Now that you have your Action Card, it's time to put it to work. The One-Minute Daily Inventory is the most magical part of implementing this system. Here's why it's special: I don't know about you, but I can get really excited to grow in an area when I read, watch, or listen to a new teaching. But then, when I realize how much work it'll take to make the change, I often give up after a few days or weeks—if I ever get started at all. Here is the problem: there is a big difference between *inspiration* and *implementation*. If you never get started or give up too quickly, you'll miss the change you were looking for. That cannot be an option in recovery. So, in recovery, I learned the secret to making growth practically automatic and effortless. It's called a *daily inventory*. I've adapted it for the Mask-Free Program into the One-Minute Daily Inventory, which unlocks the key ingredient for automatic growth and what many psychologists have told me can single-handedly change your habits: maintaining awareness.

Maintaining awareness puts growth on autopilot. That's where the Action Card comes in; we use it to perform our One-Minute Daily Inventory. Here's what you do. You ready?

*Read it once a day.*

That's it. Seriously. Read the Action Card for one minute each day, and you're done.

You probably expected this to be more complex, but it's not. Just read it once per day. Nothing more, nothing less. Don't overthink this. You don't have to write anything down. You don't have to grade yourself. You don't have to do *anything* else.

Just be present and truly read it once a day at a minimum. If you do that, you'll be performing your One-Minute Daily Inventory. Over time, your mask-free growth becomes practically automatic.

> Maintaining awareness puts growth on autopilot.

It's amazing how surprised people are when I tell them this. They assume there must be more, right? Like I have said, there is a difference between *simple* and *easy*. Remembering to do something once per day isn't easy over time. So, in order to make you successful, the inventory has to be incredibly simple. I can't tell you how many people have reached out to me to share that they read their card every day and, after a week, they started to notice a difference that only grew over time and ultimately changed their life. All it cost them was one minute per day.

Now a warning as you start your inventory: don't judge yourself if you haven't done what you've written on your card that day or if you miss a day reading it. It's not a daily test. The only goal is to maintain awareness. Each day, you may fail or be successful at living what's on your Action Card. But, if you maintain awareness, you will notice small improvements over time, and the masks practically remove themselves. After days, weeks, and months of these small improvements, you'll look back and see that you've come much further than you ever imagined. Instead of changing your life in one grand gesture (that rarely sticks), you will change it with a series of tiny, incremental improvements.

One minute is really all it takes to change your life.

**One minute is really all it takes to change your life.**

I've been doing this for seventeen years, and I've been blown away by the power of maintaining awareness. During one particularly busy season, for example, I came to realize that I wasn't making time for the most important people in my life. Specifically, I was declining their calls and not being intentional about spending time with them. I was hyper-focused on my business at the time, and those unexpected interruptions to my workday were…well…interrupting my work. As a result, I wasn't connecting with these important friends, family members, and members of my recovery community.

This started to weigh on me, so I made it the focus of my Action Card. My uncomfortable work was to connect with at least one of my loved ones over the phone or in person each day. Every night before I went to bed, I read that card and was reminded of my uncomfortable work. Some days, I realized I had taken the calls or gone to coffee and had great conversations. Other days, I declined all calls and meetup requests. After reading this card once a day for a few weeks, two things happened. First, I gradually started reconnecting with the key people in my life. Second, I realized that the days I went to bed feeling pessimistic about life were the days I had avoided talking to my key people. For the first time, I saw a correlation between talking to my loved ones and the way I saw the world. I never would have noticed that if my Action Card hadn't kept calls and connections front and center in my mind. This one act created a noticeable improvement in my quality of life every day. And all it took was one minute once a day for a few weeks. The power of one minute is remarkable.

The beauty of the One-Minute Daily Inventory is that it is short enough that *anyone* can make time for it. The danger, though, is that it's also short enough to skip or flat-out forget for two, three, or twenty days at a time. That's why I suggest adding the inventory to an existing daily routine. For years, I was inconsistent with my One-Minute Daily Inventory because I overcomplicated things by putting it on my phone calendar as a daily appointment. Every day, that appointment reminder would ding on my phone, and every day, I dismissed the alert without a thought. My daily routine was to *dismiss the alert* instead of *read my card*, so I had to change something. Instead of carving out a separate minute, I added the One-Minute Daily Inventory to a routine I was already doing. That's how I ended up reading my Action Card every day while I brushed my teeth. I was trapped there for a minute or two with nothing to focus on anyway, so I taped my Action Card to my mirror, and now I read it while I brush my teeth. Then I spit, rinse, and get my daily dose of awareness.

> **The power of one minute is remarkable.**

I have seen Action Cards implemented into other routines. I've seen people who are big readers use the card as a bookmark. When they sit down each day to read, the card is right there in front of them. I've seen people keep the card on top of their pillow, so they read it when they go to bed at night. If you watch TV every evening, you could put your Action Card next to the remote control. Some people like to put it on their car dashboard or sun visor and read before pulling out of the driveway. This is why I recommend laminating the card; it keeps it safe wherever you put it.

> **I don't know anyone who doesn't have one minute a day to make their life massively better.**

I've shown you how to distill three big principles into a simple little card. Now, you are only one minute a day away from more time, more trust, and more true leadership in your life. I know a lot of busy people, but I don't know anyone who doesn't have one minute a day to make their life massively better.

## Step 4: Start Your Recurring 28-Day Action Plan

Okay, so you did the worksheets, distilled them down into a simple Action Card, and are ready to review that card for one minute every day to maintain awareness. What's next? The next step is to do a 28-Day Action Plan.

Most addiction treatment facilities are set up around a twenty-eight-day treatment plan. Why twenty-eight days? They've found it's a particularly effective period for initiating behavior change, leaving old ways behind, and cementing new ways of living. My initial twenty-eight days in a treatment facility changed my life. Everything I've done, every relationship I've made, and every success I've experienced throughout my entire adult life has been built on top of those twenty-eight days. It helped me adjust to my new, drug-free way of life. Now, it's time for you to harness the same power of twenty-eight days to launch your new, mask-free way of life.

Over the next twenty-eight days, I want you to do these four things:

1. **Share Your Action Card:** I want to see your card. Post a picture of it on social media using the hashtag #maskfreemovement. By sharing, you'll not only inspire others in the Mask-Free

Movement (including me), but you will also take the "power of paper" one step further. Now, it's not only real; it's something you've sent out into the world for someone else to see. You aren't alone. Others are out there practicing their system every day too. There is power in sharing this for both you and them.

2. **One-Minute Daily Inventory:** Spend one minute a day reviewing your Action Card as part of an existing routine. I know the brain wants to make this more complex, but resist that urge. Just read the card to maintain awareness of what you wrote and why you're doing this.

3. **Assess Growth:** After you have done this for twenty-eight days, set aside ten minutes for a time of reflection. Take the online assessment to see quantitative progress or changes and ask yourself the questions below.

   i. What worked?
   ii. What didn't?
   iii. What did you learn?

This will prepare you to take the next step.

4. **Make a New Action Card:** Now, it's time to create a new Action Card. That's right, you're filling out the Action Card again. There is so much power in filling out this simple card. Whether you are doing the exact same card, an evolution, or focusing on a completely new mask, fill that sucker out. Read back through the Action Card instructions above if necessary. And visit www.maskfreeprogram.com for more Action Card templates.

At the end of twenty-eight days, you'll start a new 28-Day Action Plan with your new Action Card. Rinse and repeat. I told you this is about repetition. You don't stay in shape because of one really intense

**We commit one minute a day every day for the rest of our lives in order to live and lead mask-free.**

workout. You stay in shape when you work out regularly. So, to keep your mask off, you'll write a new Action Card every twenty-eight days from now on. Remember when I told you that addicts are either growing their recovery or heading for a relapse? The same is true for mask addicts. We commit one minute a day every day for the rest of our lives in order to live and lead mask-free.

## WORK THE SYSTEM CHECKLIST

Be sure to complete these four system-level steps as you begin your mask-free journey:

- ✔ Complete the 3 Principle Worksheets
- ✔ Create an Action Card
- ✔ Perform a One-Minute Daily Inventory
- ✔ Start your recurring 28-Day Action Plan

## PART 2: GET A SPONSOR

The first time you complete the 28-Day Action Plan you will get a glimpse of what your new mask-free life will look like, but you can't stop there. The second piece of this three-piece program is still missing: your sponsor.

## Get a Sponsor Immediately

As powerful as the mask-free system is, the three principles alone aren't enough to keep your mask off for the long run. We are dealing with an addiction here—a mask addiction. It's like Chuck told me near the start of my recovery journey: you can only stay clean on ego for so long. That's why you need to get a sponsor—*immediately*.

Remember, a mask-free sponsor in this program is someone who is working the mask-free system and has a sponsor of his own. With that in mind, your sponsor needs to have a little bit more experience working the program than you have. In twelve-step recovery, the rule of thumb I learned is that a sponsor should ideally be at least one step ahead of the sponsee in the steps and must have a sponsor of his own. Similarly, in the Mask-Free Program, your sponsor must meet these two criteria:

1. Your sponsor must have completed at least one 28-Day Action Plan.
2. Your sponsor must have a mask-free sponsor of his or her own.

No cheating or shortcuts here. Experience is key in this program, and you'll need your sponsor to share his or her experience working the system.

But where do you find a sponsor in this new, revolutionary, Mask-Free Program? Great question! If you have someone in your life who has already completed his first twenty-eight days in the Mask-Free Program, you can ask him to sponsor you. If someone in your company has rolled out this program (your boss, coworker, and so on) and she's already been working the program for a while, she could be a great sponsor. Or, if you are outside of a company there may be people in your community who are working this program and could be a great fit. Also, as tempting as it is to think in terms of hierarchy in your community or professional environment, it doesn't apply here. Remember what I said about the intern sponsoring the executive? All that matters is that the sponsor meets these criteria. And, if you don't have anyone around you who's experienced in this program, you can connect with a sponsor at www. maskfreeprogram.com.

I was only in the Betty Ford Center for a month, but that was enough time to see people leave, go back out into the world, relapse, and come right back into treatment. The common denominator between most of these men and women was that they did not get a sponsor once they left treatment. They thought they could do it on their own. They thought they could catch their own blind spots. They were wrong. After all, drug addicts can't see their own self-deception, and mask addicts can't see their own masks. If you can't even see it, how do you think you'll be able to keep it off? You can't. Not alone. If you're serious about keeping your mask off, you'll follow the *whole* program. That means getting a sponsor.

> **Drug addicts can't see their own self-deception, and mask addicts can't see their own masks.**

## Become a Sponsor

Once you've completed your first 28-Day Action Plan and have a sponsor of your own in place, congratulations! You're now ready to be a sponsor. Let's talk about a few specific things your sponsor will do for you and you'll do for your sponsees throughout the recurring 28-Day Action Plan. In addition to the duties we discussed in chapter 5, a sponsor in this program does three specific things:

1. Helps you reflect on your growth at the end of each 28-Day Action Plan and reviews your Action Card with you for your next 28-Day Action Plan.

2. Helps you start sponsoring others after you complete your first 28-Day Action Plan.
3. Shares his or her experience with you, points out blind spots, and answers questions along the way.

Remember, you're helping someone by sponsoring them, but that's not the only reason you do it. You do it just as much to prevent yourself from putting your mask back on than you do to help someone else take theirs off. Sponsorship is your greatest opportunity to *give it to keep it.* You're striving to stay mask-free for yourself, and it helps to know someone else is counting on you. By helping your sponsee, you're actually helping yourself. At the end of the day, your sponsee is working this program, your sponsor is working this program, and you're working this program. This program gives you the chance to help others while you help yourself.

> **Sponsorship is your greatest opportunity to *give it to keep it*.**

## GET A SPONSOR CHECKLIST

There are only two key things you need to do for the sponsorship step, but both are critical for your success:

- ✔ Get a sponsor *immediately*.
- ✔ Become a sponsor after your first 28-Day Action Plan.

## PART 3: JOIN A SOCIETY

A mask-free society is a group of people who are all working the mask-free system with a sponsor. This is a group that meets regularly—just like my twelve-step home group and meetings—and gives everyone a safe place to leave the masks at the door.

It's not enough to *belong* to a society, though; you actually have to *interact* with the society. I told you about the time I was at a work function at a bar with my coworkers. I felt completely out of place there with that group of people because I had different priorities and a different value system than they did. All I wanted to do was get out of there and meet up with my friends from my twelve-step home group. Thinking about them, texting them throughout the night, and knowing I'd have to catch up with them later was the only thing that got me through that night without feeling tempted to have a drink. Whether you're fighting to overcome drugs or masks, you need a society around you if you want to win.

> **Whether you're fighting to overcome drugs or masks, you need a society around you if you want to win.**

### Society Guidelines

Don't confuse your mask-free society with a community organization or social club with bylaws, membership orientation, fundraisers, and an official "leader." Instead, the society I'm talking about is a group of people who meet regularly to share their challenges, solutions, and experiences living and leading mask-free. For that reason, *participants should have a copy of this book and a desire to work the system with a sponsor.*

As you saw in chapter 6, the typical twelve-step meeting isn't complicated, but it is powerful. The same is true for a mask-free society meeting. In these meetings, you will have a common language and common goal. You can realign your perceptions of yourself and the world, and you can have access to infinite experience.

Here are the guidelines for the meeting:

+ Meetings are held at a regular, consistent time and place.

- Meetings use the suggested mask-free meeting format (below).
- Meetings have no designated leaders or owners. However, there *are* trusted volunteers who may take responsibility for setting up the meeting.

Meetings are crucial, but don't lose sight of why you're meeting. It's not a party, a prayer group, a whining session, or a clique. It's not about making friends or conducting business. This society is about your shared addiction to masks—period. So, the meetings are structured around that one commonality.

Each mask-free meeting should follow this simple format, giving the participants time to:

1. Share a problem.
2. Share their experience applying the program to a problem.
3. Share an experience living the program.

> This society is about your shared addiction to masks—period.

And don't forget to celebrate milestones. Celebrations are often easy to overlook, but they are a crucial part of maintaining momentum in the program. If you've been working the program for an entire year, you need to celebrate that in front of your society. Take a year-long look at what worked, what didn't, and what you learned from that year. This is a great way to see and share the incredible progress that happens by maintaining your One-Minute Daily Inventory every day for a whole year. You can also take the assessment again after a full year of working the program to spot clear, quantitative improvements in your life and share them with your society. These are the men and women who will support your efforts to keep the masks off for life. They're there to help you in the long run, and they need you to do the same for them.

**Find Your Society**

If your company or community already has a mask-free society, all you have to do is join them. But, if you don't have access to one, you can join our Mask-Free Program complete with mask-free society meetings at www.maskfreeprogram.com.

## JOIN A SOCIETY CHECKLIST

You only have two action steps for this part of the program, but they are critical to your success:

- ✔ Join a society.
- ✔ Attend regularly.

The program is now fully up and running in your life. You are now working the three-principle system, have a sponsor alongside you, and have a society of fellow mask addicts who *get it*. In the beginning of this book, I promised you that I wouldn't just tell you the *what* or the *why* and that I was going to tell you the *how*. Well, now you know exactly how to drop the mask, practice rigorous authenticity, and lead like your life depends on it!

## GROWING YOUR MASK-FREE SKILL

Living mask-free is a skill. Just like in sports, you need to practice that skill over and over to be effective. For example, pro basketball players make hitting three pointers look easy. I can study their shots and try to learn how to do that same thing. Then, I get out on the court, brick my first ten shots, and wonder why I missed. The reason the pro can hit three pointers all day and I can't is not what they do *in* the game; it's what they do *outside* of the game. It's the thousands of three pointers they shoot in practice to increase their skill level that makes the difference. They *live* the game, because it's their job. That's how you get the freedom of the mask-free lifestyle: by living it.

Remember when Chuck called me out for not working my program? I thought that I was just undisciplined or lazy, but I learned I actually lacked the clarity and energy to take simple and life-changing actions over and over. Well, in this book, we have worked the three principles that have given you a tremendous amount of clarity and reclaimed a ton of energy. I have also equipped you with an implementation plan to turn these principles into muscle memory. Now, as you near the end of the book and the start of your mask-free life, the key will be whether you can harness that energy and clarity to do a few simple things over and over. This is the difference between *learning* this program and *living* it.

That's why recovering drug addicts have a leg up on everybody else. We don't live our programs in order to become great leaders; we do it in order to live. The average leader doesn't have that same sense of urgency. As a result, leaders who *choose* to live mask-free, who approach it with a drug addict's sense of urgency, have a tremendous opportunity to become great.

> Leaders who *choose* to live mask-free, who approach it with a drug addict's sense of urgency, have a tremendous opportunity to become great.

Now, before I officially welcome you to the Mask-Free Movement, I have one last story to tell you. It's a story of warning. It's a moment in my life when everything fell apart personally and professionally. It's a moment when the pressure to wear the masks was greater than it had ever been in my recovery. And it's a moment when I stopped doing everything I have outlined in this book. If sharing this deeply personal and painful story helps just one person avoid the choices I made, telling it will have been worth it.

# CHAPTER 8

# A TALE OF TWO DIVORCES

THROUGHOUT THIS BOOK, I'VE WALKED YOU THROUGH A PROCESS for becoming and staying mask-free in your work and life. I've talked about my recovery from drug addiction. I've talked about how the principles I learned in recovery set me up to win big in my career. I've talked about how living and leading mask-free is the single greatest competitive advantage you can imagine. I showed you the power of the Mask-Free Program, complete with the system, sponsor, and society, and I've given you a plan for implementing the most important parts of a good recovery process into your own life and leadership. So, as we near the end of this book, what's left for me to tell you?

> In one year, living *with* a mask cost me my business, and living *without* a mask cost me $1 million.

I want to tell you about the time I took everything about living and leading mask-free that I've unpacked in this book ... and threw it out the window. I spent nearly a year retreating back to my masks, and I paid dearly for it.

In one year, living *with* a mask cost me my business, and living *without* a mask cost me $1 million.

Unpacking my worst year since getting clean in detail may not sound like the happiest ending for this book, but I want you to learn from what I've been through. A sponsor's number one job is to share his experience living this program. In this book, I am sharing my experience, and that means being open about my highs *and* my lows working this program. This story has plenty of both.

## TWO TIMES I SHOULD HAVE SAID NO

By early 2014, I'd been the CEO of InQuicker for almost four years. We had millions in revenue and had a team of thirty people. Professionally, I was flying high, but I still felt the pressure of taking InQuicker to the next level. I knew we needed an experienced sales leader to help us get there. That's when I hired Angie.

Hiring Angie (not her real name, by the way) is a great example of me *not* doing the uncomfortable work I needed to do. As I considered the needs of an experienced sales leader, I became intimidated by the process of vetting and hiring an employee of a significantly higher caliber. So, when Angie came strongly recommended by a trusted advisor, I decided to shortcut the hiring process. I didn't create a job description. I didn't evaluate other candidates. I didn't dig too deeply into her background. I avoided the uncomfortable work and, in the process, did the bare minimum. In short, I violated every rule on how you should hire a leader to your team.

Of course, I did interview Angie, and she impressed me early on. After the third interview, though, I got a sense that something was off. But we were desperate for strong sales leadership, and I was so busy that the *last* thing I wanted to do was to take the time to start a new process to hire someone. Plus, I was insecure about my ability to hire the right person, so I pretended I knew what I was doing, ignored my instincts, and hired her anyway. I convinced myself that she was great, that my advisor was right, and that I was wrong. I hid my hesitations behind a mask. It was the first of many mask mistakes I'd make that year.

That mask only got thicker when I presented Angie to the rest of the team. I beamed with confidence as I talked to my team about her. I enthusiastically went on and on about her qualifications and what she could do to help us grow. My confidence was contagious, and my key leaders got excited about Angie joining us and taking over the sales team. We didn't know it at the time, but that was the beginning of the end for life as we knew it at InQuicker.

Here's the problem: I had a strong gut feeling that Angie was a bad hire before I brought her on board, but I ignored it. To hide my misgivings, I put on a mask of confidence and acted like Angie walked on water. That made my leaders see Angie how I *wanted* them to see her, so they, in turn, ignored the red flags they saw. My mask caused each of them to put on a mask, and we all

> The mask epidemic has a domino effect.

hid our concerns from ourselves and one another. After all, an advisor we all trusted vouched for her, so she couldn't be all bad, right? As it turned out, though, he only knew her personally; he had never worked with her professionally. However, because he knew we needed to fill the position and she seemed good for the role, he put on a mask and pretended he knew Angie better than he did. I've learned over the years that masks lead to bad information, and bad information leads to bad decisions. This was the prime example. My advisor put on a mask, so I put on a mask, so my leaders put on a mask. Apparently, the mask epidemic has a domino effect.

This wasn't the first time in recent memory when I ignored my instincts and hid my doubts behind a mask. Five years earlier, I'd done the exact same thing. Only that time, my doubts weren't about a potential hire; they were about a potential wife. Today, I am very happily married to my incredible wife and partner in life, Elizabeth. But, back in 2009, right around when I started at InQuicker, I was in an unhappy marriage to my first wife. I don't say that to hurt or insult her. We just weren't a good match, and we both knew it.

Hiring Angie gave me the same feeling of doubt and uncertainty that I had on my wedding day with my ex. In both situations, I doubted what my instincts were telling me and thought calling them off would make me look weak. In hiring Angie, I talked her up so much and convinced everyone else how great she was that I was terrified of admitting my doubts. With my ex, I didn't want to look foolish or embarrass her in front of our family and friends on our wedding day. It's amazing how two completely different situations, one personal and one professional, can feel the same way internally. I could have bailed on the wedding. I could have bailed on the hire. I *should* have bailed on both, but I went through with them. In both situations, I tightened the strap on my mask, hid behind the painted-on smile, and went through with what my gut was telling me was wrong. These were the two most dramatic examples in my life of saying yes when I could have said no. But, in both situations, I was letting my mask call the shots.

> I was letting my mask call the shots.

## TWO MASKS FOR THE PRICE OF ONE

I offered Angie the sales leader job in February. After the honeymoon period wore off, I started to worry that it was a bad fit. She simply didn't *get* our culture, and she stood out like a sore thumb among the tight-knit work family we'd created. To make things worse, by May, we were far behind on our sales projections. I began to doubt she could actually do what we hired her to do. I got much more concerned when she started playing politics in the office. In a one-on-one meeting with me, she started asking strange questions about my partner and cofounder. She asked, "Where is Dylan? He's never here. Is he committed to this business?"

I cut her off practically mid-sentence. "Let me stop you right there. Dylan's my partner and my friend. We *built* this together, and we *run* it together. We are one team, so please don't ask me that again." That wasn't the response Angie wanted. She brushed it off and acted like she was only asking out of curiosity, and I assumed that would be the end of it. It wasn't.

Less than a week later, I noticed Angie in Dylan's office. That was unusual. From that point on, though, I started seeing Dylan and Angie having a *lot* of one-on-one meetings. It became clear that she was trying to insert herself between me and Dylan. When I shut her down, she had apparently moved on to Plan B: she aligned herself with Dylan and against me. I never imagined he would let her do that. I was wrong.

> The "no politics" culture we had created was under siege, and I was not happy. This is *not* what I wanted InQuicker to be.

As it turned out, Angie wasn't good at selling our service to hospitals, but she was *great* at selling her value to Dylan. She had immediately sniffed out his blind spot—he couldn't see the business benefit to strong workplace relationships—and she used that against me. In my years as CEO, I had spent what some might call an extreme amount of time, energy, and money loving our team. From my perspective, building this kind of safe, mask-free society was the number one reason for our rapid success. My partner was a facts and figures guy and never fully bought into the concept. When Angie started complaining to him about how much we were "wasting on things that don't matter" and about how we needed "to operate like a *real* business," it had a visible effect on him.

By late spring, we were way off on our sales goals. I'd been watching Angie closely, and it was clear she would not be able to get us to that goal. Not only was she ineffective at selling and creating a sales strategy, but I was also hearing rumblings that the people who reported to her *really* didn't like her leadership style. She embodied the no-emotion, no-personality, all-business, corporate middle manager that most of us had fled from. At one point, she even chewed out someone on our finance team for asking a salesperson a simple question. The "no politics" culture we had created was under siege, and I was not happy. This is *not* what I wanted InQuicker to be.

So, by midsummer, I knew it was time to make some changes. To hit our sales goals and protect the company culture I'd worked so hard to create, I decided to let her go. Before I did, though, I wanted to give Dylan a head's up. In our next meeting, almost as an aside, I said, "Listen, we're not on pace to hit our numbers and we're having some leadership issues on the sales team, so I'm thinking about letting Angie go or at least putting her on a performance improvement plan." I was moving on to the next agenda item when my partner cut me off.

"No."

"No, what?" I asked.

> I was paying a terrible price for the mask I'd allowed myself to put on when I hired Angie.

"No, you're not going to let Angie go, and you're not putting her on a plan," he said. "Angie isn't the problem. You are. You aren't doing what I need you to do as CEO. In fact, I'm going to put *you* on a performance improvement plan, and I'm thinking about replacing you as CEO."

I was stunned. He and I had always had very different styles, but he had trusted me to run the company for years. My entire strategy was built on heavily investing in relationships with employees and customers. Amazingly, Angie had managed to convince him that my emphasis on the relationship stuff was the very thing that prevented us from having the growth he wanted. She had successfully wedged herself between us and convinced Dylan that InQuicker's greatest weakness was *me*.

In just four months, this new employee—who I *knew* I shouldn't have hired—had broken my longstanding relationship with my business partner, started corrupting the mask-free society we'd built at work, failed to improve our sales by any meaningful metric, caused employees to start hiding their own fears and frustrations behind new masks, and somehow managed to convince the majority owner that all of this was my fault. I was paying a terrible price for the mask I'd allowed myself to put on when I hired Angie. And, the longer I kept it on, the higher that price seemed to get.

> With each new hit, I retreated further and further into my masks.

## A BATTLE ON TWO FRONTS

After years of riding high at InQuicker, my work life was turning into crap while, at home, my ex and I struggled to make our marriage work. After years of effort, one near-divorce, and one trial separation, we finally threw in the towel and officially filed for divorce in February 2014—the same month I offered Angie the job. As we started the divorce process, it became clear that the biggest issue would be how much of my ownership in the company my ex would get. Because our company was on the cutting edge, it was difficult to determine the value of my equity. As a result, our marital dissolution process was going to take longer than either of us wanted while our lawyers tried to work it out.

Moving into summer, I was neck-deep in my divorce negotiation, fighting to keep my ownership in the company I had built, and was in direct conflict with my business partner, who was now threatening to remove me as CEO. With each new hit, I retreated further and further into my masks. I brought the tough-guy "you can't hurt me" mask to my divorce negotiation meetings. I wore the "I won't let you do this to me" mask in front of Dylan and Angie. And my team members, who desperately needed me to be real with them, only got the "everything's fine!" mask. I was scared, hurt, angry, frustrated, and lonely inside. Everything around me was out of control, and I had no stable ground. I stopped practicing rigorous authenticity. I tried to control the uncontrollable and constantly obsessed over the outcome. I avoided the uncomfortable work left and right. As I retreated into my mask, I stopped doing the very things that had helped me get what I was now fighting to keep. I didn't let anyone see the real me that year. As the pressure built, it was like I had forgotten everything I'd learned about recovery. Falling back into my old drug habits was never an issue, but I certainly fell back into my old mask habits. I knew from experience that lingering there too long could kill me, so something had to give. But things were about to get even worse.

## LEVERAGE VS. LOYALTY

As things unraveled at work, I became an absent leader. I couldn't face my team. I felt like I couldn't tell them why I was letting Angie ruin our culture or that Dylan was planning on removing me as CEO. I was stunned by the turn of events and didn't even know how to deal with it, let alone explain it. Plus, I planned on fighting for my leadership role, and I didn't want to drag the team into the mess. Here I had built this beautiful society around authenticity, vulnerability, and connection, but now I couldn't share these painful parts of my life with the society. I felt incredibly isolated. It tore me up to be around them without being real ... so I just stopped being around.

As I worked through the conflict with Dylan, our meetings turned into regular hostage negotiations—and my compensation became the hostage. Since I wouldn't be CEO anymore, he wanted to cut my salary by 60 percent. Additionally, he demanded that I waive a clause in my contract that protected me from having my ownership diluted to practically nothing. These negotiations were exhausting.

After multiple conversations in which I made it clear that I would not waive my anti-dilution clause nor accept such a drastic pay cut, he told me that if I didn't agree to his demands, he would just sell our company. I couldn't believe it. He knew I had told our team we would never sell, and he knew I was going through a divorce. Now, he was using both as leverage. There was even a moment when he pointed out how selling the company during the middle of my divorce would complicate my negotiations with my ex-wife. To me, it seemed like something out of a soap opera.

> Because I had put *my* masks on, they had retreated back to *theirs*.

In one intense exchange in the conference room at our office, I was so hurt, so taken aback, that I said, "I am absolutely stunned right now. I have always valued loyalty over leverage, and I have been loyal to you for five years. But now, it appears you value leverage over loyalty." He didn't disagree.

I stumbled out of that conference room and looked around at the team I'd built. I loved every one of them, but I felt like a stranger to them. I was their friend and leader, and I was engaged in the fight of my life just a few feet from their desks, but they didn't even know it. Even worse, they were fighting their own battles. I wanted so badly to save them, but I couldn't. Over the last few months, as I isolated and retreated into my bunker, I had abandoned them. They had been left to fight the war for our culture without me . . . and they were losing. Fear, anxiety, uncertainty, and distrust had taken root. Our open, loving environment had been replaced with something the rest of us hardly recognized. Because I had put *my* masks on, they had retreated back to *theirs*. Now, in contrast to the revolutionary, countercultural workplace I'd sold them on, we were all

you can do: Tell Dylan to go for it. Tell him to go ahead and sell if that's what he wants to do."

I hated the suggestion and replied, "Then I'll lose my company. How does that solve anything?"

They replied, "It's simple. You will be the buyer."

I didn't understand and said, "That would be awesome, but how can I be the buyer? I don't have the money."

"That's the cool part," they said. "We'll help fund it. We believe in your company, and we believe in you. Go call his bluff, and he will either back down or put the company up for sale. If he does that, you can buy it, he will be out, you can fire the troublemaker, and you will have your company back."

> **Because I had finally pulled off the masks and let a trusted society see my true self, fears and all, I came across the solution I so desperately needed.**

It was genius. Pure genius. In a matter of minutes, Dylan's leverage had become mine. If he backed down, I could go back to leading my company. If he went through with the sale, I could just buy my company. Suddenly it didn't matter what Dylan decided to do.

I can't explain how I felt in that moment. I had felt so incredibly alone, but it turned out I wasn't. I had just been hiding behind my mask. It was like I'd been stumbling around in the dark for months looking for a light switch and then, with a click, someone lit up my whole world.

The freedom I felt in that moment of revelation was incredible. Because I had finally pulled off the masks and let a trusted society see my true self, fears and all, I came across the solution I so desperately needed. I left that group meeting energized and ready to fight. It all came back to the system, sponsor, and society. Remembering what I had learned, I started living the three principles:

+ I **practiced rigorous authenticity** by thoroughly examining myself for every new mask I had put on over the past several months. It was clear there were several.
+ I **surrendered the outcome** by seriously considering what I *couldn't* control and what I *could* control. I couldn't control whether Dylan chose to sell, but I could control if I raised the money to be the buyer. I couldn't control that my team was fighting a cultural battle with Angie and Dylan, but I could control if I dropped my masks and led the team through it. By focusing only on what I could control, I reclaimed more energy and peace than I had all year.
+ My **uncomfortable work** then revealed itself. I had to have the difficult conversation with Dylan and call his bluff. Then I had to have difficult conversations with my team and explain why I had been MIA.

I started my uncomfortable work with Dylan. He and I were scheduled to have an offsite meeting to discuss my response to his ultimatum. This was the first time during this whole ordeal that I sat down with him feeling perfectly calm, comfortable, confident, and detached from the outcome. Dylan jumped right in, telling me that I needed to take the pay cut, accept dilution, and step down as CEO. If I didn't, he reiterated, he'd just sell the company. When he was finished, I calmly looked back at him and said, "Go ahead and sell the company if you want. My answer is no."

He was shocked. He kept arguing with me and, when he realized I wouldn't budge, he said, "Okay, then. We need to find an investment banker and start the process to sell InQuicker." I could tell he was serious. My business partner was asking for a divorce—my second one that year.

But here's the thing: I was a drug addict who had fought back against the hell of addiction by practicing rigorous authenticity, surrendering the outcome, and doing uncomfortable work. Those principles taught me that the goal in life isn't to win or lose. The goal is to live mask-free. And, in this case, I had to surrender a company and a marriage to do it. This wasn't about what I wanted to do or how much I wanted to make; it was about who I wanted to be.

While that relationship was falling apart, I went about my second big area of uncomfortable work: rebuilding the society I had allowed to crumble. Everyone at InQuicker was in duck-and-cover mode. Angie had taken over more and more of the company by then, which meant morale was down and attrition was up. My COO, Kurt, would be the first person I'd talk to. We had built the company together.

> The goal in life isn't to win or lose. The goal is to live mask-free.

He was a friend whom I loved dearly and the rock of our company. I knew he was wondering what was going on. After a leadership retreat, I pulled him aside and told him everything. I laid every mask I'd been wearing at his feet. I worried that he wouldn't respect me anymore. But, when I was done, he just hugged me and asked, "How can I help?" And together, we set out to take our company back.

Afterward, I went to employees individually and did two things. First, I apologized for being absent over the past few months and for not being the leader they needed me to be. Second, I told them that I was working on a solution to our problems and asked for their trust and patience. I didn't tell them all the sensitive details, but I shared enough for them to get the bigger picture of what was happening. After all, this was *their* company too. They had helped build it just like I had, and they missed what we had once been.

I recently asked my friend Stacie, one of my leaders who stuck with me back then, what she thought during the whole ordeal and specifically when I finally showed her my real face again. She said, "In that moment, I felt like I could drop the managing-perception mask I'd felt forced to wear that year. I'd spent so much time trying to look like I was okay with everything going on, to look stronger than I really was, and I was exhausted. I just remember sitting there as we talked that day thinking, *Thank God. Michael is back. Whatever's going on and whatever's going to happen next, at least I know that Michael is back with us.*" There was so much healing in that season of sharing. One by one, I could see masks dropping off every face. I could *see* my friends again. I could *be seen* by them too.

## DOUBLE DIVORCES

It didn't make sense for us to hire a new CEO if we were going to sell the company soon, so I kept the title (even though Dylan had stripped me of most of my authority). Angie didn't take that news well. It appeared that she thought *she'd* be the next CEO. After working so hard to wedge herself between us, she wasn't getting the prize she wanted. I tried (unsuccessfully) to hide my smile as Dylan broke the news to her.

> One by one, I could see masks dropping off every face. I could *see* my friends again. I could *be seen* by them too.

Everything picked up steam throughout the fall. Even though I was CEO in name only with no real power, I was able to spend more time with the team and travel on sales presentations. As a result, our sales rebounded bigtime. I don't know why I was surprised that our success would start thriving again once I stripped my masks off. The mask always wants us to believe that things are better with it on.

My divorce agreement was progressing during that time as well. Because my ex wanted a portion of my business equity, we had the company valued and I made her an offer to buy out her portion of my equity at that valuation. It would mean trading in every dollar of my cash reserves to buy my equity back, plus I would be in debt to her for years, but I wanted to double down on myself and my team.

All this brings us to one fateful day in November—probably the single biggest day of my life. My ex and I had a meeting to sign our divorce papers before lunch. We met at the office building, amicably signed the agreement, and formally dissolved our marriage. As agreed, she would make no claim to my equity in InQuicker, and I would pay her the amount determined by the valuation we had performed. Clean and simple. Divorce number one—check!

> The mask always wants us to believe that things are better with it on.

After lunch, I arrived at an office building down the street to meet with Dylan and our investment bankers. We were there to sign the papers to officially put the business up for sale. Everything up to this point had been preparation; this meeting was when it all became very, very real. This was essentially the point of no return. I met Dylan in the lobby and, as we walked up, I said, "Are we really going through with this?" He said yes, but I still half-expected him to back out at any second. He didn't. The bankers walked us through the paperwork and details, and Dylan started signing where instructed. No hesitation, no further questions, nothing. He signed and then passed the papers over to me. This was really happening. Divorce number two—check.

## WOULD YOU PAY $1 MILLION TO STAY MASK-FREE?

The next order of business in that meeting was to discuss the company's valuation. Our investment bankers had done a thorough analysis of the market and had arrived at an estimated value for what they thought the company would sell for. When I heard the number, my heart dropped into my stomach—not because it was low, but because it was 600 percent *higher* than the value we used in the divorce papers I had signed just two hours prior. My ex and I had gone through a nine-month divorce process and endless negotiations and had finally settled on an agreement where she sold me her portion of my equity. And now, two hours later, I found out that she was only getting one-sixth of the cash she would have gotten if we'd signed the papers just one day later.

I should have been thrilled at the high valuation. That meant my stake in the company was worth far more than I had hoped. But it also meant my dream of buying the company myself was out the window. There was no way I or my friends could afford to buy the business at that price. It dawned on me that I wasn't going to be able to keep my company after all, and I was going to have to break my promise of never selling to my team and give up the company I loved.

Regarding my ex-wife, it meant I had a major decision to make. We had made an agreement that was negotiated in good faith. Should I now tell her that she had just sold her equity to me for one-sixth of its value? It didn't take any time to decide. I wasn't going to let the mask win. I decided to tell her.

> I wasn't going to let the mask win.

My friends begged me not to do it. They even staged an intervention on me—a nice throwback to my active drug addiction days. If this had happened a few months earlier, maybe there's a chance I would have hidden the information behind one of the masks I'd picked up. But I was done with that. That's not how I wanted to live, and it's not who I wanted to be. So, again, I worked the system:

- I **practiced rigorous authenticity** by being honest with myself about what my gut was telling me and about the mask I felt tempted to put on. I *knew* the right thing to do—at least for me in that situation—was to tell my ex. Anything else would have been a violation of my personal values.

- I **surrendered the outcome** by letting go of what I couldn't control—the actual value of the company and how much more money I might have to pay her—and by focusing on what I could control, which was being true to myself and sharing the news with her.
- I **did uncomfortable work** by having the conversation with her.

That's right: I actually told her the company's value was six times higher than we thought, meaning her divorce settlement should have been six times higher than she agreed to. Then, I asked her if she wanted to draw up new papers using the updated figures. Of course, she said yes.

So, rather than writing her a check and keeping my full equity in the company, I did the only thing that was true to my authentic self: I gave her a significant stake in my company. Not ideal, to be sure, but it was the right thing for me to do. I never doubted for a second that I had to live mask-free in that moment—even when that decision cost me $1 million six months later.

## THE BIG FINISH

My whole attitude was different after that day in the investment bankers' office. It was like the universe had sent me a colossal test of my recommitment to live and lead mask-free, and I felt like I passed. I was reminded that, if I could be real in such outrageous circumstances, I could do it in *any* circumstances. This completely changed my perspective as I went back to work to face my team, my partner, and Angie.

With Angie still in control of sales, her team members were jumping ship. We lost five people by mid-December, and I heard rumblings that several others were going to use the holiday break to start looking for other jobs. It was clear to me that there'd be no way to salvage our culture with Angie still there. However, for some reason, she remained protected by Dylan. I knew I didn't have the clout with him to fire her, so I took a more practical approach. Because so many people were leaving, Kurt and I asked our HR company to do exit interviews with the former employees. Right before we all left for the holiday break, the HR company set up a call with Dylan and me to report their findings. They walked us through all their data and gave us the bottom line: from their HR perspective, Angie was a terrible manager and was creating an enormous amount of liability for our company. I asked what they recommended. Their answer was quick and clear: "We recommend you terminate her as soon as possible."

> **If I could be real in such outrageous circumstances, I could do it in *any* circumstances.**

Dylan and I talked afterward, and he was blown away. He had just been confronted with what the rest of us had known for the better part of a year, that Angie was putting our entire company in jeopardy. With more than a little satisfaction, I said, "Dylan, can I *please* fire her now?"

His answer: "Yes." It was music to my ears.

At that point, I was still CEO in title only. I hadn't actually run my company for almost a year. So, I reminded Dylan that, as our majority owner, he was about to enter a process of selling his company without a leader of sales, without its historically strong culture, and without a number of employees who had quit (or were about to). I told him that, at this rate, there wouldn't be much of a company left to sell. Shaken, he asked me to fully take the reins as CEO again.

I said no.

This got his attention. I said, "I'm not going to clean up your mess under these conditions. The only way I will come back is if I can lead *my* company *my* way with *my* people. And I won't promise to stay through the acquisition. I will only stay if my team and I get to pick the buyer to make sure everyone has the best experience possible through the transition. This team and our culture are the reason we even have a company to sell, and we need the freedom to get back to what makes InQuicker great."

He agreed to all of it. He had no choice, really. He wanted to sell the company, and he needed the team that had made it so valuable over the last six years to stay. It was time to get back to work and, when we came back from the winter break, my first order of business was to fire Angie. Our first day back, we sat Angie down in the conference room with just Dylan, me, and HR. I explained that we had hired her to accomplish a clear set of objectives and that she had failed to do the job. I had all the documentation to back it up. Then, I said the phrase I'd wanted to say for ten months: "I'm afraid we're going to have to let you go. Do you have any questions?"

> **This team and our culture are the reason we even have a company to sell, and we need the freedom to get back to what makes InQuicker great.**

"Just one," she said. "Dylan, what do you have to say about this?" She was counting on a last-minute save from her benefactor.

"Nothing," he replied.

With that, Angie realized her blanket of protection was gone. The HR person started walking her through the details, and I walked out of the room … smiling.

I spent the rest of the day having incredible one-on-one meetings with each team member, telling them that Angie was no longer with the company and apologizing for everything that had happened all year. I'd apologized before, but they weren't totally sure they could trust me then. Now, they knew my masks were really off and it was safe for them to take theirs off again.

Our company and team had been through the wringer, but we managed to start the year off on a high note. Over that first week back, I reached out to the employees who had recently quit to apologize to them and let them know that the "problem" had been resolved. Much to the delight of the rest of the team, two of those key employees, Stephanie and Julie, agreed to come back—as long as we could assure them they'd be returning to the InQuicker we all knew and loved. At a company offsite soon after New Year's, I told the team I wanted to introduce them to the two new awesome salespeople I had just hired. Then, Stephanie and Julie came in and the whole group went nuts in celebration.

Later that day, Dylan and I held a roundtable discussion with the team and did a mini-post-mortem of the year. Honoring the trust they'd given us again, he and I both took responsibility for what we'd put them through over the past year. I was proud of Dylan that day. He stepped up and owned his mistakes in front of everyone. That went further with them than even he realized at the time. When they saw Dylan, of all people, dropping his masks, they got the signal loud and clear: we finally had our company back.

> They knew my masks were really off and it was safe for them to take theirs off again.

A few months later, Dylan and I started serious negotiations with a publicly traded company and finally came to an acquisition agreement. True to his word, Dylan gave me right of approval on the buyer, so I was able to guarantee jobs for the employees after the sale. I even managed to secure a chunk of the proceeds—millions of dollars—to give the team. Our investment bankers later told us they had never seen a company be that generous with their team. It just felt like the right thing to do. After all, they were our competitive advantage; there's no way we were doing the deal without giving them the chance to share in the profits. We closed the sale late summer 2015, and each person came out a winner.

A year earlier, I was going through a rough divorce, being edged out of the company I had built, dealing with an attempted coup by a bad hire, and feeling betrayed by a friend and brother I'd built a business with. Every time I took one of those hits, I retreated back behind a mask—just like I'd done so many years ago as an active drug addict.

the team that I loved, and the ability to truly lead myself. Sure, thanks to living mask-free, my reworked agreement with my ex-wife cost me $1 million, but in return, I got something money can't buy.

The real value of dropping my mask was that it showed me in concrete terms how powerful the whole notion of masks and authentic leadership is. By leading mask-free, I had grown my company from nothing to nearly eight figures in six years. Then, I almost let it fall apart by hiding behind a mask for a little over six months. Once the mask was back off, we were not only able to heal the company but were able to sell it for six times more than I expected. Why? Why did this lone healthcare startup demand such a high price? It's because of our people—our motivated, relational, awesome people.

**Yes, our product was revolutionary, but it wasn't nearly as revolutionary as our mask-free culture.**

Yes, our product was revolutionary, but it wasn't nearly as revolutionary as our mask-free culture.

## PAVING THE WRONG ROAD

People want to be leaders because they want success. They believe the money and influence that comes with success is going to make them happy. But then, to protect this leadership persona they've created, they end up hiding themselves, just like I did. In trying to reach heaven, they end up paving the way to their own private hell one brick at a time.

We all run the risk of caging ourselves in the hell of success, but authentic, mask-free leadership is the way out. It means freedom not only for you, but for the people you lead and the people that follow them. The value in connecting on a true, unobstructed, face-to-face level with the people you lead is without parallel. This isn't just a management skill; it's a life skill. It's not just a professional skill; it's a personal skill. It's not just a skill for leading; it's a skill for living. And, once you learn this skill, it is yours to keep forever. You'll never want to give it up—even if it costs you $1 million.

# AFTERWORD

FOR A DRUG ADDICT, ACTIVE ADDICTION INCLUDES LYING ABOUT who we are, manipulating the way the world sees us, and controlling the way we feel at any expense. We're hurting ourselves and the people we love in pursuit of the next high.

The leaders of this world are facing their own addiction—and *their drug of choice is the mask*.

If you are struggling with hiding your true self behind a mask, there is a way to take it off and keep it off, a way to find your freedom leveraging the power of the Mask-Free Program and its system, sponsor, and society.

> The leaders of this world are facing their own addiction—and *their drug of choice is the mask*.

In our time together as you have read this book, just as the drug addict has been equipped to fight their drug addiction through the twelve steps, you have been equipped to fight your mask addiction.

And make no mistake about it. IT. IS. TIME. TO. FIGHT.

But, as you embark on your new mask-free life, I want you to think long and hard about why you are doing this. Yes, you will gain a competitive advantage. But I want you to think about what Archie asked me early in my recovery:

**What if you lived your mask-free life, and all that happened was that you helped one more person remove their mask?**

"What if all you get is the ability to help just one other addict get clean and learn this way of life? *Just one.* Would that be enough?"

*What's your enough?* What's your measurement of success? What if you don't gain more time, trust, and true leadership? What if you gain no external advantages at all?

What if all the world achieves is one more:

- Executive saying no despite the pressure to say yes.
- Manager embracing difficult conversations they once avoided.
- Front-line employee sharing their unique perspective.
- CEO declaring their weaknesses to their teams instead of hiding them.
- Entrepreneur no longer pretending to be stronger or happier than they are.
- Parent no longer wasting their time and energy on things that won't matter on their deathbed.
- Child growing up knowing how to live mask-free.

What if you lived your mask-free life, and all that happened was that you helped one more person remove their mask? Just one?

I am telling you … *it would be enough.*

If you are an addict, I want you to know your addiction isn't a stigma; it's a freaking superpower.

If you are a leader, I want you to know that the *worst* thing about you just might be the *best* thing about you.

And to you, the person reading this book right now, I know there is a great leader inside of you. But if you want the world to see it, you will have to do what drug addicts do.

# ACKNOWLEDGEMENTS

I USED TO GLOSS OVER ACKNOWLEDGEMENTS. NOW I UNDERSTAND why authors write them. I poured my heart and soul into this book, but, like anything else I have done in my life, it never would have happened without a team.

I want to thank Hannah Paramore for encouraging me to write this book and for connecting me to my publisher, Jonathan Merkh and Forefront Books, without whom this wouldn't have been possible.

Allen Harris: You aren't just an editor. You are the best co-writer in the world. You worked so hard to understand the nuances of what makes this book special and your combination of grace and conviction were exactly what we needed. I am so grateful for you.

Jeremy Snow: You spent countless hours in a busy season of your life helping pull the right stories out of me for my TEDx talk which became the number one TEDx Nashville talk of all time, and, as a result, we got to work together on this book. You helped me understand my mission better than I did. I am eternally grateful for you and your unique perspective.

Stacie Pawlicki: Thank you for living the InQuicker journey with me and taking a chance on a thirty-something drug addict back in 2010. Thank you even more for your partnership in launching the Mask-Free Movement and for your tireless effort in bringing out the very best in this book. Your unique perspective was invaluable in this process.

Pam Lass: Thank you for your mentorship. Thank you and Steve for being incredible friends and fans. Thank you even more for helping us start the Mask-Free Movement.

Kate and Charlie: For your generosity in answering the many questions and freak-out moments as I attempted to tell our story.

Jess Smith: You committed yourself to this story being told when no one else did.

My blood family of Mom, Dad, and Brooke: This boy became an addict and you still loved him. You gave me the gift of life and the gift of recovery. Thank you from the bottom of my heart.

Chuck: Your passion for recovery and generosity in sharing your experience is rare even in the rooms. I hope this book shows you the impact you have made on the people around you. I know no matter what happens in my life, the rest of my life, you will be there.

Momma Holly: You have taught me so much, but above all you have taught me unconditional love. Your grace, wisdom, and humanity make you an asset to any recovering addict or human who is lucky enough to be loved by you. This addict is the luckiest.

Toby: Thank you for being a fellow spiritual warrior on the path. God never fails to flow through your words, and I cherish our friendship. This life, book, and movement would not have been possible without your encouragement.

Erica: You are the closest friend who has been there for the good, the bad, and the ugly before my addiction, during it, and after. The love I have for you cannot be explained and I know we will never stop being friends the rest of our lives.

To the entire InQuicker team: There were a million stories I wanted to tell about each of you that didn't make the book, but I hope we will continue to love one another and tell these stories the rest of our lives. There are too many of you to thank but I am so grateful for all of you. You guys are the real stars in the InQuicker story.

To my homegroup: You guys are my tribe. I love you so much. You are truly home.

To Anne, Aaron, and the Davis crew: You tolerated me when no one else would and you loved me when no else could. I am so grateful for you guys and will love you the rest of my life. To Aaron especially: you kept me off the streets and provided me food and shelter even when I was stealing from you. You are my brother.

To my daughter, Amorette: In less than one year, you have stolen my heart. You are perfect simply as you are. I hope you never hide who you truly are.

To my beautiful, brilliant, funny, and relentless wife, Elizabeth: You are the reason this happened. You believed in me and this message even when I didn't. You practically willed it into existence. We have spent thousands of hours in our home working on everything from the very first keynote to the book to this movement. There isn't an element of what we are doing that wasn't made possible by you. What an honor it is to not only live with you but work with you. Your material contributions in every phase over the last four years are the reason that we are here. And you managed to do all of this while giving birth to our beautiful daughter, Amorette, becoming the best mother on this earth, and remaining an incredible wife. I never in my life thought it would be possible to respect, love, and adore someone this much until I met you. You are truly my partner in all things in life, and in success or failure, you remain the reason I am the luckiest man in the world.

To my higher power whom I choose to call God: Thank you for my addiction. Thank you for every hard moment, bad relationship, and tragedy. Thank you for the enormous mountain of fertilizer. I love you, and I am so grateful to be loved by you.

# MEET MICHAEL BRODY-WAITE

AT THE AGE OF TWENTY-THREE, Michael Brody-Waite was a full-blown drug addict. Every day he drank a fifth of vodka and a twelve-pack of beer, he smoked two packs of cigarettes and more weed than any human should, and he did whatever other drugs he could get his hands on. He had been kicked out of college, fired from his job, and evicted from his apartment. He had no money and no home, was throwing up blood, and believed he would be dead before his thirtieth birthday.

Then, on September 1, 2002, after running out of options and fearing death, he checked into rehab, entered recovery, and has been transforming himself every day since.

Michael's TEDx Nashville *YouTube* video, "Great Leaders Do What Drug Addicts Do," is the number one talk in the history of TEDx

Nashville. It has been seen by over one million people in over twenty-five countries and provides insight into his seventeen-year journey from addiction and near homelessness to successful entrepreneurship. This talk sparked the #MaskFreeMovement and brought awareness to Michael's Mask-Free Program, built on three principles inspired by his recovery, showing leaders how to achieve balance, reclaim energy, and thrive in work *and* life.

In 2010, Michael left a Fortune 50 company at the height of the recession to cofound and lead InQuicker, a healthcare SaaS company that allowed patients to self-schedule appointments online. Under his leadership, the organization grew to 20,000 percent revenue growth in less than six years. This exceptional growth landed InQuicker a spot on the *Inc.* 500 list of Fastest Growing Private Companies. Additionally, the organization was named one of the "Best Places to Work" four times and recognized as Healthcare Company of the Year. In 2015, InQuicker was sold to a publicly traded company. After selling his company, Michael served for three years as the CEO of the Nashville Entrepreneur Center, a 501c3 that helps over 2,000 entrepreneurs every year start or grow a business.

Michael is an acclaimed speaker, *Inc.* 500 entrepreneur, award-winning, three-time CEO, a leadership coach, and an author. His accomplishments include being named Most Admired CEO, named to the Top 40 Under 40, and being recognized by the Nashville Chamber of Commerce as Healthcare Entrepreneur of the Year.

Today Michael is on a mission to teach individuals, organizations, and communities how to lead themselves by living mask-free. In his personal time, he is focused on being the best husband, father, and recovering addict he can be. For more information, please visit www. MichaelBrodyWaite.com to learn how the Mask-Free Program can help you or your organization thrive.

# FREE GIFT FOR YOU

With reading this book, you get FREE access to
the Mask-Free Program, which includes:

**Mask-Free System:** Exclusive content,
worksheets, action cards, videos, and other
updates from Michael.

**Mask-Free Sponsor:** Connect with a
sponsor who will help you as you work the
Mask-Free System.

**Mask-Free Society:** Join a society with
others who are working the Mask-Free
System and share challenges, solutions, or
experiences.

**Go to maskfreeprogram.com to sign up now!**

**Connect with Michael on Social Media**

Facebook: https://www.facebook.com/michaelbrodywaite/

Instagram: @MichaelBrodyWaite  https://www.instagram.com/
michaelbrodywaite/

LinkedIn: http://www.linkedin.com/in/michaelbrodywaite

YouTube Channel: youtube.com/michaelbrodywaitechannel

TEDx "Great Leaders Do What Drug Addicts Do"
youtube.com/watch?v=UUnRKf2CemA

SpeakerHub: speakerhub.com/speaker/michael-brody-waite

# PRAISE FOR *GREAT LEADERS LIVE LIKE DRUG ADDICTS*

Michael Brody-Waite authentically shares his wisdom in a captivating and practical way. Anyone who wants to become a better leader will benefit from reading this book.
**Daniel H. Pink, the #1 New York Times bestselling author of When, To Sell Is Human, Drive, and A Whole New Mind**

Eliminating the nonessential masks that hold us back is key to becoming a great leader. This is brilliantly illustrated in this new book from Michael Brody-Waite.
**Greg McKeown, author of the bestselling New York Times and Wall Street Journal book Essentialism: The Disciplined Pursuit of Less**

By sharing his deeply personal experiences and his Mask-Free Program, Michael is inviting us all to live up to our unique potential. As Michael says, this isn't a program for those who need it. This isn't a program for those who want it. It's only a program for those who do it. Thanks to Michael, my leadership team and I have seen first-hand the benefit of practicing rigorous authenticity, surrendering the outcome, and doing uncomfortable work. We'll be forever grateful.
**Lisa Gevelber, Vice President of Global Marketing, Google**

From my experience leading at the highest levels of our military to tragically losing a beautiful son to an accidental drug overdose, Michael elegantly describes what underpins success in two seemingly disparate disciplines: recovery from drug addiction and leadership. Practicing rigorous authenticity, accepting what one can and cannot control, and totally committing to execution enable true success in either endeavor.
**Admiral James A. "Sandy" Winnefeld Jr., retired United States Navy admiral, ninth Vice Chairman of the Joint Chiefs of Staff, and Co-Founder of Stop the Addiction Fatality Epidemic (SAFEProject)**

Michael's story is uncomfortable, provocative, and ultimately inspiring. It will encourage you to put aside your own masks and armour and take the great risk in fully showing up as who you are in your life and your work.
**Michael Bungay Stanier, author of the bestselling book The Coaching Habit, Founder of Box of Crayons, and named #1 2019 thought leader in coaching**

Addiction is more often associated with destruction than with redemption. In Michael Brody-Waite's case, he has suffered both the destruction of addiction as well as the redemption of recovery. And, he has used his journey to hone life and leadership principles that guide everything he does. His experiences and learnings have helped him become a successful entrepreneur, a much admired and trusted leader, and a humble, grateful human being.

> John Ingram, Chairman, Ingram Industries Inc. Board of Directors, Chairman of Ingram Content Group LLC, Philanthropist, and owner of Major League Soccer Team, Nashville SC

An incredible read. Michael demonstrates how the principles drug addicts use to recover can give any leader a competitive advantage and reinvent leadership as we know it.

> Marshall Goldsmith, 3-times New York Times bestselling author of What Got You Here Won't Get You There and Triggers (recognized by Amazon.com as two of the Top 100 Leadership & Success books ever written). Rated by Inc. as America's #1 executive coach and the only two-time winner of the Thinkers 50 Award for #1 Leadership Thinker in the world

This book is inspiring and empowering because it is TRUE. Written by a man that has successfully led two different companies, authentically. I am inspired by Michael's fresh approach to leadership.

> Cordia Harrington, Founder and CEO, The Bakery Cos. and named #16 of 25 Top Women Business Builders by FAST Company

DON'T start reading this book before bed because you won't be able to put it down! And, I'm warning you, it touches a nerve … early and often. Here I am thinking I'm living my life authentically when Michael makes me realize I've got a trunk full of masks that I wear, each creating barriers to my happiness and my impact in the world. This is a must-read for anyone seeking a "breakthrough" strategy to be the best version of themselves.

> Sherry Deutschmann, Founder and CEO, BrainTrust, CEO Sunset Ventures, Inc., and named 2016 White House Champion of Change by President Obama

*A vulnerable and insightful read about a revolutionary approach to leadership. Michael demonstrates how the "mask-free" principles drug addicts use to recover can give any leader a competitive advantage and reinvent how we think of leadership.*

**Shervin Eftekhari, President, Zander Insurance Group**

*This is such an inspiring and thought-provoking read. "Mask-free" living is such a fresh take on leadership and relevant no matter where you are on your leadership journey.*

**Jay Chawan, Co-Founder and Chief Financial Officer, Guy Brown**

*Michael Brody-Waite lived a lifetime before the age of 30 and survived, barely. In his book,* **Great Leaders Live Like Drug Addicts,** *he exposes his own scarred truth in order to get all of us to release our, as he calls it, masks, and live up to our own full potential. I've known Michael for many years in many capacities and the one word that describes him best is "real." This book is real; it's his realness that opens our eyes to our own. It's time we all got a lot more real and stepped out from the curtains and removed our masks. Michael brings you a full-on rollercoaster ride to help you slow yours down. Dig in and get real.*

**Andy Bailey, CEO, Founder and Head Coach of Petra Coach and bestselling author of There Is No Try**

*I've known, been inspired [by], and challenged by Michael Brody-Waite for many years. The first time we met, he told me his remarkable recovery story. And over time, he's given me important life and business advice that has been grounded in this work. I don't have addiction issues. Yet, using the recovery techniques I've learned from him has helped me personally and professionally.*

**Bob Bernstein, restaurateur and owner of Bongo Productions**

# GIVE YOUR PEOPLE A
# LIFE-CHANGING EXPERIENCE

MICHAEL TEACHES INDIVIDUALS, ORGANIZATIONS, AND COMMUNI-ties how to lead themselves by living mask-free. At his events participants are equipped with the tools and instruction on *how* to achieve balance, reclaim energy, and create more success in work and life.

Michael's offerings include:
- ✦ Keynote Speaking
- ✦ Workshops
- ✦ Corporate Coaching
- ✦ Guest Appearances

Everyone can benefit from living and leading a mask-free life. Michael has shared this message with entrepreneurs, executives, students, small businesses, nonprofits, universities, and Fortune 100 companies.